Military Philosophy

Attention Authors

'We Convert Fighters into Writers'. That's the motto of Manas Publications since more than four decades. Our message to the world is that India can win the battle not only by the bullet but also by the pen. There is no dearth of intellectuals in our country, but their knowledge is confined to them only. No sincere effort has been made by any other publisher to channelise their knowledge in national interest. That is why the talent of a large number of intellectuals remains latent. An author transforms his knowledge into a manuscript, and it is our job to spread his/her knowledge by converting it into a beautiful book. For over four decades, Manas has been motivating the intellectuals by publishing their manuscripts and would like to publish your manuscript too. If you or your colleagues have any manuscript ready for publication or are working on it, kindly contact us with detailed synopsis and list of contents. We will transform your work into a valuable publication. If you wish, we can also suggest you the suitable subjects for writing the books related to your area of expertise. Manas is known for its publishing quality and commitments. We take utmost care in production and give wide publicity to the book as well as its author through our national and international distribution network.

Military Philosophy

Cdr SV Chavannavar (Retd)
Indian Navy

Manas Publications
(We Convert Fighters into Writers)
New Delhi-110002 (INDIA)

MANAS PUBLICATIONS
(We convert Fighters into Writers)
(Publishers, Library Suppliers, Importers & Exporters)
4402/5-A, Ansari Road (Opp. HDFC Bank)
Darya Ganj, New Delhi-110 002 (India)
Off: (011-23260783, 23265523, Res: 011-23842660
Fax: 011-23272766
E-mail: manaspublications@gmail.com
manaspublications@yahoo.com
Website: www.manaspublications.in

ISBN: 978-81-7049-493-5
₹ 495/-

Designed at
Manas Publications

Printed in India at
Rajdhani Printers, Delhi
and published by Mrs Suman Lata for
Manas Publications, 4402/5-A,
Ansari Road, (Opp HDFC Bank),
Darya Ganj, New Delhi-110 002 (INDIA)

Contents

Part II - Aspects relating to personnel

Part III- Combat philosophy

Part IV - Other related issues

Prologue

(Portrait of a soldier as an Activist)

"An army of principles can penetrate where
an army of soldiers can not"

- Thomas Paine

I regard my admission to the National Defence Academy at Khadakvasla as the legitimate beginning of my military career not only because I was legally bound to pursue a career in the Indian Armed Forces but also because I was being exposed to some kind of juvenile 'military ethos' for the first time. This ethos was essentially rudimentary in nature and comprised of certain Do's and Don'ts and some quotes of convenience which served as behavioural justification. The cadets' concept of camaraderie, integrity and soldierly behaviour were contained in these. Proclamations like "Everything is fair in love and war" and "A man who fights and runs away, lives to fight another day" were often heard as loudly as Gen Chetwode's prescription of leadership. I observed this code without much conviction.

Later, on being commissioned in the Indian Navy, I realised that officering (leadership) is an individual activity. I, therefore, felt the need to equip myself with internal resources to meet the challenges of this individual task. One of these was to establish a simplistic code of conduct in the form of Do's and Don'ts to guide me in my day to day functioning. Some of my early experiences were not only unsavoury, but also shocked my conscience. I do not wish to relate those episodes as it may sound like belly aching. However, I earnestly continued my endeavours in that direction.

As a junior officer, I once submitted an article titled "Military Ethics" for publication in *Naval Dispatch*, the official in-house magazine for furtherance of professional knowledge. The article was promptly returned with amplifying remarks that articles relevant to naval profession are welcome. I was shocked. My next article in the press on 'Jurisprudence in the Armed Forces' earned me a princely honorarium of Rupees two hundred and fifty and the Commander-in-Chief's displeasure. Many well meaning seniors advised me that it was good writing in bad taste. I was amused. These instances of rejection steeled my resolution to strive for acceptance. Towards the fag end of my naval career, while working in a training establishment, I was encouraged to indulge in this hobby horse. I was elated. This brief monograph is the product of that indulgence.

Book writing is a hobby horse which you ride across an obstacle course for the sheer joy of completing it. It is also cathartic to the author as he unburdens himself. In this case, my endeavour is aimed at the greater common cause - that of facilitating the evolution of an ethical code of conduct for the uniformed fraternity. I, therefore, consider myself as a Soldier turned Activist because of my conviction and commitment to the cause. However, due to ritualistic stringency of security a soldier may dare to write on a subject matter like this only as post retirement activity. Having sheathed one's sword one may wield the pen. Whether pen is mightier than the sword is for the posterity to decide.

When Solomon Tauber, chief protagonist of Odessa File committed suicide in desperation, an unrelated Peter Miller took up cudgels on his behalf, but for reasons of his own to track down the Nazi criminals. Activism like any other ism will find supporters from quarters expected and unexpected.It is my ardent hope that the cause this book espouses will find support from all quarters—military, polity, bureaucracy and citizens in general. It can only strengthen the foundations of our democracy and enhance the efficacy of our Armed Forces.

Preface

"Adam was the only man who, when he said a good thing, knew that nobody had said it before him"

- Mark Twain

Use of Preface Long winded prefatory notes while not indulging in expression of authorial indebtness to a large number of individuals, are beacons that aid the reader to navigate through the ensuing monograph. Such notes chart the parameters within which the monograph is to be understood and interpreted. They also enunciate the ground rules for evaluating the same. More uninitiated the reader to the subject, greater is the usefulness of such notes.

Scope & Nature of subject The title of this book 'Military Philosophy' may sound preposterously glamourous expression for a mere 'ethical code of conduct' or a set of Do's and Don'ts for the practitioners of the profession of arms. Justification for elevating the subject to that exalted status is borne out by the nature and scope of the subject. The vista of the subject is wide and may be roughly described in terms of the levels at which soldiers operate. The highest echelon being the politico-military level where the preponderant focus is on the role and methodology of functioning of the armed forces in relation to the body politic and other vital institutions of the democracy. At the administrative level, the subject dwells on aspects relating to the "man behind the machine". At the tertiary or lowest level, it deals with conduct in the battlefield or combat area and may be appropriately termed as "combat philosophy". The hierarchy indicated above are not rigid boundaries nor are they directly related to the rank structure of the armed forces.

Military philosophy is not a poetic view of the profession of arms, yet a quest in the realms of poetry may provide useful insights into the profession and the subject.

A knight ther was, and that a worthy man
That from the tyme that he first bigan
To riden out, he loved chivalrye
Trouthe and honour, freedom and courteisye

- Chaucer in *Canterbury Tales*
(Fourteenth Century)

Theirs is not to reason why
Theirs is but to do and die

- Lord Alfred Tennyson in
Charge of the Light Brigade
(Nineteenth Century)

Those that I fight I do not hate
Those that I guard I do not love
Nor law, nor duty bade me fight
Nor public men, nor cheering crowds

- W B Yeats in An Irish Airman forsees his Death (Twentieth Century)

An important inference that may be drawn from the above quoted samples of poetry from different periods is that the moral or ethical values for soldering are guided by contemporary values. Yet as in other affairs, past influences the present and both past and present coalesce to evolve the futuristic. Therefore excessive indulgence in nostalgia of 'our times' and 'those days' by the old time veterans may be construed as their inability to comprehend the dynamics of military profession.

Military philosophy can not be strictly regarded as an applied field of study although it has its moorings in other subjects like political science, moral philosophy, religion, and management as also other value systems. In fact, the discipline has not so far received the focussed attention that it deserves, as it has been expedient to apportion or hive off reflections on Military Philosophy to other disciplines mentioned above. This is perhaps because of our favourable inclination towards precise and definitive disciplines in consonance with scientific temper of our times. Analysing the military profession is a formidable task because it involves imaginative, speculative and reflective thinking. The other difficulty is that the military profession does not reveal itself to superficial inquiry. A great deal of introspection and insider view are necessary. While the process is irksome to the soldiers, the academics are indifferent.

Necessity of the subject At the lower echelons of the military, the defence personnel have an impressive way of performing their tasks. In all their drills including operation of their equipment, crisp and clear executive orders evoke quick and obedient responses and prompt completion reports. The visible demonstration gives the onlookers of military environment an impression that the guidelines for functioning of a soldier are stated in totally unambiguous terms at all times. However, what is apparent is not always true. Soldiers are at times required to function under very trying circumstances. Under such circumstances, a soldier who is unaware of the ethical norms or code of conduct for practitioners of military profession drifts like a twig in the torrents if he is diffident or behaves like a runaway horse with its harness if he is confident. In either case he is erring on the wrong side. The result, of course, is that he is a potential victim of court martial or other disciplinary action, which is of personal consequence to the individual and failure in the performance of his vital duties, which is of concern to the society. Such situations arise because of ambiguity or multiplicity of views in his functional areas. Soldiers at all levels have to tread these grey areas of varying shades and are vulnerable to errors of judgement. The situation is further aggravated because the profession of arms hardly provides its incumbents the time for armchair reflective thinking. The heat and din of combat further reduce the reaction time. Even in non-combat zone, a soldier is required to respond spontaneously if not instantaneously. Under such circumstances, thorough knowledge and understanding of the professional ethics by the soldier is the only insurance of righteous conduct.

It is rather paradoxical that while human endeavours in pursuit of excellence have ushered in professionalism; the word itself is often employed to convey a narrow restricted meaning. The term is generally used in day-to-day parlance to mean excellence in the professional skill, where as the word has much wider connotation. All pretensions to professionalism must satisfy three qualitative stipulations - ability to perform a function (knowledge and skill), promote some professed virtue or societal good (aim) and have an ethical code of conduct for the practitioners of the profession (philosophy). While no claims to professionalism can be sustained without the former, the noble aim of body military is taken as axiomatic. On this universal axiom rests the assumption about the nobility and virtuosity of the profession of arms. These two criteria at times tend to overshadow the importance of an ethical code of conduct oblivious of the possibility of a soldier covering himself with ignominy in the performance of his duties. While military philosophy equips the soldier with knowledge of functional methodology of this vital institution and his honourable role, awareness of the subject is essential to the ordinary citizen as well. It will enable him to judge and evaluate the performance of this powerful instrument of state policy.

Reasons for Apathy Military matters do not engage the interest of many. Even the uniformed fraternity does not bother itself with all aspects of the profession. That perhaps is the bane of narrow professional specialisation. Survey of defence related writing reveals two distinct streams. Higher direction of war, Nuclear Issues and diplomacy being written by academics and soldiers pursuing campaign studies and memoirs. Military ethics does not find favour with both streams because it is not regarded as hard core study and receives only episodic treatment. There is also the dampening effect by the military establishment itself which regards individualistic thinking and questioning attitude as inimical to the interests of discipline. But apathy of polity to defence matters and national security is deplorable. The nationalist leaders who led the non-violent freedom movement regarded the armed forces as an inevitable appendage. Subsequently too, in a nascent nation in a hurry to build its economy, industrial/technological base, political structures and social development, the armed forces were neither imagined nor envisaged as contributing to developmental activities. Their image as non-productive, resource consuming activity has made them the neglected constituency.

Aim of the Book The work is an analytical description of the military profession and other related issues to facilitate and encourage speculations to evolve an appropriate military ethos. It is hoped that this book will encourage defence writers to explore areas other than traditional ones. Citizens should evince greater interests in military matters so that defence studies thrive in non-military academic institutions as well.

Style of the book

> *"If you have an important point to make, don't try to be subtle or clever. Use a pile driver. Hit the point once. Then come back and hit it again. Then hit it a third time, a tremendous whack"*
>
> **- Winston Churchill**

The author regards this book as a pioneering work in its domain and therefore, is written in the style and spirit of intellectual activism. The author has cautiously restrained himself from adopting the Churchillian model. Even while adopting a courageous stance or view point, articulation has been subtle or suggestive because evolution of any value system needs to be nurtured with care and responsive attitude. The information or knowledge content may be rudimentary for that is how all pioneering works begin but reflective speculations and authorial stance attempt to stimulate fresh thinking. There are no startling revelations either—sensationalism is inimical to deliberations of this kind.

The belief that an inferior mind discusses individuals, average mind events and superior mind issues, overlooks the fact that very often the three are inextricably intertwined. In this book there is no wanton iconoclasm, events are viewed without prejudices and issues discussed in the spirit of academic indulgence. The process of obtaining enduring core values is longwinded and labourious but is rewarding.

Author's approach Certain propositions in the text may seem like extremes of viewpoint and at an impractical distance from ground reality. The attitude is justifiable because fidelity response of any concept or proposition needs to be tested across wide spectrum before being accepted as norm. Due to intricate nature of the issues and numerous possibilities, the approach has been suggestive and not prescriptive to the extent possible. A subject with so many diverse issues may appear like pastiche of the disperate. An attempt has been made to maintain readability by sequential arrangement of topics. If there is a resonance of repitition in the text, it may be viewed as reiteration of an important issue or as necessity to maintain contextual coherence.

Book writing is rarely accomplished through spontaneous spring of wisdom, on the contrary the process is much akin to Military Intelligence, involving collection, collation, synthesis, analysis and interpretation. It is only naivete to regard such a process as totally original and creative. Further, no systematic research has been done on the issues dealt in this book as is obvious by conspicuous absence of references and end notes. The author is acutely aware of his vulnerability to charges of plagiarism. An acknowledgement by the author that all inputs have been internalised and acceptance of moral responsibility for all evaluations of personalities, events and issues should satisfy the advocates of systematic library research.

Bangalore *Cdr SV Chavannavar (Retd)*

Introduction

"Our scientific power has outrun our spiritual power. We have guided missiles and misguided men"

- Martin Luther King

The above quote reflects the paradox of human condition today. While material prosperity has ostensibly ushered in better quality of life, the spiritual core has ossified into insensitive mass. Individual, familial and societal values have become inconvenient baggage of yesteryears. The institutions which fostered these values have become the cloak rooms of abandoned baggage. Civilisations which were shackled to religion as an eternal source of strength have broken their moorings and are adrift. Parochial nationalism has emerged as the new religion and soldier its icon.

This soldier is a product of narrow specialisation in the age of rising professional classes. Such professionals in pursuit of their specialisation with blinkered vision need a professional code of conduct and contemperaniety the key element. Military as an institution assiduously train their members to equip them with knowledge of warfare, its techniques and associated skills but pay scant attention to indoctrination to instill moral attributes. It is perhaps this lacking which prompted snobbish gibe by Tallyrand - "War is too serious a matter to be left to military men". Conscience of statesman has also failed us much too often thus prompting Charles De Gaulle to modify the observation - "Politics is too serious a matter to be left to politicians". French are perhaps too critical. We may rationalise and complete what Tallyrand left unsaid - "War is much too serious a matter to be left to military men, but war without soldier's sanity is vunmitigated disaster".

Military Philosophy is concerned with facilitating understanding of the nature of issues involved in the profession of arms. Its vista is a confluence of knowledge from diverse domains - some of them definitive subjects like social sciences, management, legal and constitutional realms and others speculative like religion, humanism and rationalism. Customs and traditions which play an important role in this profession is another stream that contributes to the subject. Such an amalgam can be anything but a definitive guide. Therefore, a soldier armed with this knowledge, devises his guidelines in an act of balancing between the commands of his superiors and the dictates of his conscience. In the ultimate analysis, the individual alone is responsible for his acts of commission and omission. Of course, he will be judged in accordance with the prevalent norms. It is imperative that his actions are always deliberate and not passive or evasive. A soldier must have the courage of conviction to face the consequences of his actions, be it reward or retribution.

The evolution of a professional code of conduct can not be a theoritical framework nor can it be a product of merely imaginative speculation. It has to be based on analysis and evaluation of events and conduct of individuals. It blooms in conflicting environment and is evaluated by contemporary values. Canons of military ethics have to be heard loud and clear through the din of war, cacophony of parliamentary debates and roaring public opinion. It will have to be sanctified in the defence institutions of higher learning.

A number of issues are deliberated upon in this book to facilitate evolution of an ethical code of conduct for practitioners of the profession of arms. These deliberations are divided into three parts. The division is not too rigid. It is for reasons of covenience and to deal with issues at varying levels. Military is an important institution of democracy and society. Its linkages with the society are many. In this book we deliberate upon the interactive interfaces of military with other important institutions in Part I. Some activities in the politicomiltary domain are also included in this part. Members of the body military are regulated through service conditions and established norms of behaviour. Awareness of these matters is necessary to understand the military profession. Some of these aspects relating to the 'Man' (woman included) are discussed in Part II. The issues discussed are not exhaustive but illustrative. Battlefield is the ultimate place of employment for soldiers. Their conduct in that domain is of great importance to the military and the society. Part III of the book deals with combat philosophy. Military ethos is the common thread that runs through the entire functional domain of the armed forces. Some aspects which seem remote and unrelated also influence or are influenced by the military ethos. It is for this reason that two such important issues are deliberated upon in Part IV of the book.

Part-1

Military and institutional relations

Part I - Military and institutional relations

Chapter 1: Politico-military relations

Chapter 2: Resume of politico-military relations in India

Chapter 3: Higher direction of defence (war)

Chapter 4: Military and Media

Chapter 5: Military Jurisprudence

Chapter-1

Politico-military relations

"At the root of all but the most primitive or most celestial organisation there must lie the sanction of force.......... it is not itself the foundation of society...................it is only one factor out of many which go to constitute a political community.......... But as yet no community of any degree of complexity has succeeded in existing without force, and the manner in which that force is exercised and controlled will largely determine the political structure of the state"

-Professor Michael Howard in his book
'Soldiers and Government'

Military is a profession to its members and an important institution to any political community (state) irrespective of the form of governance. However, parliament, military, judiciary and media are analogically regarded as four pillars of Indian democracy. While the latter two institutions function as 'watchdogs', the functional mode of the former two is proactive. Military as an institution is a double edged sword and therefore, the nature of interactive interface between polity and military is crucial for the political stability of the state. Antiquity of these two institutions compels retrospection of politico-military relations. In a modern nation state, the constitution of the state is the guide for these relations. There are also some maladies that occur in this domain. All three aspects mentioned above have been deliberated upon in this writing.

Historical Perspective

> *"History is the essential corrective to all specialisations"*
>
> **Sir Basil Liddell Hart in**
> ***"Why don't we learn from History"***

Survey of history of civilisations reveals that any community which did not make adequate provisions for its territorial security was run over if not totally annihilated. Therefore, military in its mutant manifestations has been an integral part of human civilisation as much as use of armed force an ancient practice. However, for the purpose of this study, it would be adequate to draw generalisations based on episodes or events that constitute a watershed in the evolution of politico-military relations rather than gleaning the entire history of mankind and attempting to date every event. Three important considerations for evaluating the state of politico-military relations are:

a. the status enjoyed by the military as an institution of the state as also the status enjoyed by its members in the society.

b. the roles assigned to the military by polity or society or the role asserted by the military itself.

c. The working of interactive interface between bodies polity and military.

The term 'military' in this chapter generally refers to Army. Air Force was the last of the armed forces to be commissioned. The nature of force wielded by Navy and Air Force did not permit them to be influential or significant players in this domain. Although there is an instance of Air Force officer having led a military coup, it was more an exception than high probablity.

Dr. Sarva Daman Singh in his book '*War*' asserts that first forerunner of military was the force for protection and acquisition of pastoral rights in agrarian societies. Sometime around Vedic period in India, the military had attained certain level of professionalism. A caste based class of professionals called Kshatriya (warrior) had emerged. A code of conduct for the practitioners of profession of arms had also evolved. Reviewers of European history trace the beginning of military to the hired men who bore arms as a means of livelihood and owed allegiance to the chieftain who suitably rewarded them. They were employed for protection and acquisition of territorial assets. These men lived on the fringes of civilisation and were often social outcasts. An important feature of such forces was their mercenary attitude. These men had no worthwhile code of conduct. This situation continued till almost the beginning of nineteenth century, except for a spell of Roman history when military was powerful element of politics.

Kingship as a mode of governance constitutes a watershed in the evolution of politico-military relations. King was both an administrator of state and supreme commander thus combining the roles of polity and military. His efficacy and success depended on his administrative ability as well as his prowess in the profession of arms. Therefore, it would not be incorrect to trace the origin of the concept 'war as an extension of politics by other means' to the days when kingship was in vogue. Prussian writer Clauswitz only formalised the concept at a later date. Military enjoyed an exalted status through association with kingship. During this period certain moral standards for the practitioners of the profession of arms were established, although they mainly related to personal qualities of the combatants like bravery, chivalry, self-sacrifice, personal honour and loyalty to king.

Increased economic interaction between countries culminated in creation of maritime force for protection of trade. It is worth noting that in early days even piracy had state sanction.The military also played the role of propogators and defenders of faith. In some societies it was used as an instrument of nation building and agent of socio-economic change. However employment of these roles did not significantly affect the politico-military relations.

"But war's a game, which, were their subjects wise,

Kings would not play at"

The above statement of 18th century poet William Cowper was rather prophetic. With emergence of new egalitarian political ideologies and forms of governance political power was transferred from aristocracy to the commoners. There was segregation of polity and military with both streams attaining professionalism. This was also the beginning of the present day politico military relations.Formation of nation states based on these ideologies imparted nationalistic character to the military serving their own flags as distinct from military as an entity owned by the king. This ushered in changes in the ethos of combatants. In our times national security has developed into a complex domain to include a host of national activities, although territorial security remains the main concern and military its chief and last resort instrument for implementing state policies. Despite the complexity, polity and military are the dominant players in the domain. Clauswitzian dictum on war is the most succinct statement on means and ends relationship between the two institutions. If war is continuation of political activity by other means, then the following logical deductions are possible:

a. Military is essentially a specialised instrument of state policy in the hands of polity.
b. Military is subordinate to polity.
c. Military is an instrument of last resort (unless state policy advocates militarism).

This, then is the foundational basis of politico-military relations except in cases of kingship and Military rule. In the former instance both the roles are combined and in the latter instance polity is obviated. Constitution of the state lays down the functional methodology.

Constitutional basis

"We must get away from the fallacy of legal solubility of all problems. In a constitution, what is left unsaid is as important as what is said. Our constitutional equilibrium can be preserved only by obedience to the unenforceable"

-Nani Palkivala
Eminent Constitutional Jurist

While Clauswitzian dictum provides the rationale for civil supremacy, constitution of the state is expected to provide the functional methodology and guidelines for establishing stable politico-military relations. Constitution is often regarded as the mother law because it goes beyond being a legal statute. It enshrines the political philosophy of state, ideals to be pursued and means and methodology to attain them. It also defines roles and functions of some important organs of state and guides inter-relationship between them. Some aspects are stated explicitly while some are implicit because even the lengthiest of constitution may prove to be inadequate framework of rules. Therefore, any interpretation must satisfy both the letter and spirit of the constitution.

As mentioned earlier, the military (armed forces) apart from being part of the governmental machinery, is also an institution in itself and an important institution of democracy. Therefore, the scanty reference to the armed forces in the Indian Constitution is disappointing but not surprising. Such gross neglect of the armed forces and callous disregard for national security has its origin in reasons historical. During the colonial rule and prior to independence, the Indian nationalist leaders were exposed to self rule though in a limited way. Even then defence and foreign policy matters were imperial subjects and therefore, India did not inherit anything by way of institutionalised defence thinking. The deliberations of the Constituent Assembly were, therefore, by and large ignorant of the enormous complexities of defence and national security. Indian Nationalist movement was not only non-violent but its leaders MK Gandhi and Nehru were successful in isolating militant leader Subhas Chandra Bose. Even after independence annexation of Hyderabad state and countering the first assault on Kashmir were regarded as police action in pursuit of internal security. Under such circumstances no better response could be expected.

Yet, it is possible to begin the quest in the dreary constitutional realms to establish the status, roles envisaged for the armed forces and basis for politico-military relations. The sole mention of the armed forces in the Indian Constitution is in Article 51 to nominate the President of India as the Supreme Commander of the Indian armed forces. This notional gesture is of symbolic significance. All important institutions in a democratic framework are notionally placed under the Head of State to avoid concentration of power in any one individual or institution. They also enjoy a degree of functional autonomy so that no institution or individual causes functional discomfiture to others. However due to dual status of military as an institution as also a governmental instrument, the Defence Minister exercises functional control over the armed forces. Status and functional autonomy are not the only considerations while seeking to establish institutional interactive interface.

The roles assigned to these institutions or organs are of far greater significance. The preamble to the Constitution is the ideal place to search for institutional responsibilities. It must be clearly understood that preamble is not part of legal framework, hence, legally not enforceable. Due to its permanence, it is also not amenable to amendment in terms of Article 356.

Many constitutional commentators regard preamble as containing the basic structure of constitution due to its pre-eminence. However, this study prefers to regard it as comprehensive mission statement. The preference for management lexicon in this overwhelmingly legal domain is because it provides prescriptive description of political philosophy of Indian state and the ideals or objectives to be pursued.

The institutional means to achieve these ideals is obvious

Justice - Judiciary

Liberty - Media

Equality - Parliament (through practice of adult franchise)

Sovereignity, Unity and Integrity - Armed Forces

Preamble

WE THE PEOPLE OF INDIA, having solemnly resolved to constitute India into a SOVEREIGN, SOCIALIST, SECULAR, DEMOCRATIC, REPUBLIC and to secure to all its citizens:
JUSTICE, social, economic and political;
LIBERTY of thought, expression, belief, faith and worship
EQUALITY, of status and opportunity; and to promote among them all;
FRATERNITY assuring the dignity of the individual and the unity and the integrity of the nation.

Of the four important institutions enumerated above, media lacks cognisable organisational structure but enjoys maximum functional autonomy and minimal governmental control. Autonomy and independence enjoyed by these institutions reflects the spirit of Indian constitution. Yet, the functional reality is different due to practical and good reasons. Since parliament represents 'we the people' it is regarded as the first amongst equals. The other reason for its pre-eminence is that though parliament is a legislative body, it also contains within it the political executive which is an instrument of implementing state policies. Here it is worth noting that the military is the last resort for the same purpose. Most writings on constitution choose to regard Executive as an important organ of the government along with parliament and judiciary, but the military, which is an important institution of democracy, is treated as any other government department. Unwillingness of Indian polity and opposition from bureaucracy to admit echelons of military into the political Executive for Higher Direction of War stems from this dichotomy. Any further deliberations on the subject, in all likelihood, will be diagnosed as belly-aching by a defence writer.

The earlier mentioned four institutions are expected to not only perform their clearly assigned roles but also maintain smooth interactive interface with each other to ensure efficient functioning of state machinery. In extreme situations when any of these institutions show signs of derailing, then other institutions react with zeal and at times cross their functional boundaries in order to set on track the erring institution. When such a corrective action is initiated by the media, it is often termed 'crusade' (used as a transferred metaphor and has no religious connotation whatsoever) and similar action by the judiciary is called 'activism'. Zealous behaviour on the part of armed forces is called 'praetorianism'. However, when the parliament is hyperactive, it can be called pandemonium' and at times 'vandalism' (based on trends in parliamentary conduct).

Even the zealous behaviour by institutions like judiciary and media may amount to nothing more than voice of sanity or expression of opinion for they possess no cutting edge faculty (lacking in wherewithal to enforce their judgement or opinion). The recent coalition action by media and civic society (anti-corruption movement of Anna Hazare) which could coerce the parliament, was the only exception. It is only the armed forces which possess this faculty. In the next writing that follows interference or confrontation by the armed forces is discussed as a malady in the politico-miltary domain, but that is only conditional. Supremacy of civil rule should prevail subject to legal validity of the civil rule and rectitude of the institution.

Functional Modes of Institutions in Democracy

Ideal	Responsible Institution	Normal FunctionalMode	Zealous Behaviour
Justice	Judiciary	independent	Activism
Liberty	Media	Free	Crusade
Equality	Parliament	----	----
Sovereignity Unity Integrity	Armed Forces	Apolitical	Praetorianism

Another important aspect of politico-military relations is that the Defence Minister who exercises functional control over the armed forces is also a member of a political party in power. However, the armed forces espouse no political philosophy and maintain apolitical stance. They owe allegiance to the Constitution of India. Therefore the constitutional basis of politico-military relations may be summarised as follows. Armed forces are an apolitical institution of democracy whose notional head is the President and the Defence Minister exercises functional control over them.

Maladies in the domain

> *"Societies are orderly and peaceable only in so far as they have solved (the) double problem, of the subordination of military force to the political government, and the control of a government in possession of such a force by legal constraints and popular will"*

- Professor Michael Howard
in *'Soldiers and Government'*

Conceptual clarity regarding supremacy of civil rule and unambiguous interpretation of constitutional basis of politico-military relations may not render the domain or the society peaceable. The apparent clarity, on many occasions, is fouled by ground realities. Under such circumstances the applecart of inter institutional relations is upset by either overzealous military or arrogant polity resulting in conflict or confrontation. Some of the maladies in the domain are discussed in general terms.

Praetorian tendencies

"When Nehru goes, the government will become a military dictatorship - as in so many of the newly independent states, for the army seems to be the only highly organised centre of power"

- Aldous Huxley writing in 1961

The phenomenon where military wrests political power is known as praetorianism (derivative linguistically not valid but adopted by the author for syntactical considerations). The term itself has been analogically derived from Roman history where praetorian guards wrested power from the praetor (emperor or military chief). In common parlance, it is known as military rule or military law or military coup. The phenomenon is wide spread - there have been more than hundred incidents of praetorianism and an equal number of unsucessful attempts in the later part of twentieth century. Geographically large and populous as well as small and scantily populated countries have been victims. It has occurred in ex-colonial states and also in states with no colonisation past. Seemingly modern and also backward countries have had this experience.

The situation has been treated as a malady in this writing based on the premise that democracy is the most evolved and egalitarian form of governance. However, circumstantial colouring can alter perception of the phenomenon. For instance it is worth recalling the occurrence of the phenomenon in the neighbouring state of Pakistan. Although the Americans vociferously cried 'foul' in the immediate aftermath of the coup in which Musharaf seized political power from the then

Prime Minister Nawaz Sharif, they subsequently toned down their criticism to accomodate both the usurped and usurper on the same political spectrum by comparative evaluation of bad democracy and good military rule (whatever it meant). And America is an elite democracy! Domestically too, Musharaf's regime had public support (although the size of this segment was not ascertained). After being disillusioned by successive corrupt civilian rule, the people of Pakistan were hopeful that Musharraf would cleanse the system.

Wide variations in the victim states and differences in perception of the phenomenon suggest use of the term 'praetorianism' in a genuine sense. Just as organic growth depends on environmental conditions, certain ambient conditions like socio economic situation, political and cultural reasons induce 'praetorianism'. Some of such conditions are:

a. The society is engulfed in socio-economic turmoil with little hope of recovery.

b. There is breakdown of political system and/or deterioration of law and order situation.

c. The civil administration is weak and ineffective.

d. The ruling head is perceived as malevolent dictator

e. External powers are keen to install a favourable government for geo-political reasons.

f. Democratic values have not taken roots in the country.

When such conditions prevail in any society, the disappointed citizens tend to regard military as a possible and better alternative due to their apparent image as disciplined and efficient instrument of state policy. It is only too late when both realise that civil administration is not amenable to methods of military management.

The nature of military rule is also very characteristic. It does not take kindly to dissent and political activity is fettered. In such stifling environment democratic values do not bloom making it extremely difficult for return to civil rule. Economically too it is disastrous for the country. Military as the custodian of state treasury expends substantial portions of revenues for improving their own conditions of service and acquisition of military hardware. Such extravagance sets the country on a path of economic insolvency. There is also gradual transformation in the state's philosophy of governance (apart from abandoning democratic norms) The state shifts its moorings to value systems more in consonance with their rule like religious fundamentalism or sectarian politics or extremism of other kinds. However, the most dangerous characteristic of military rule is its nature of self perpetuation. A soldier who has wielded unfettered political and military power is unwilling and unlikely to give up power and return to barracks. It is aptly described in the prophetic statement of Indian correspondent Inder Malhotra, who on being asked as to who would be the next ruler of Pakistan after Ayub Khan promptly replied "whoever happens to be the Chief of Army Staff at that time".

Political communities can initiate some measures to minimise the risk of praetorianism. Since the armed forces are an important and last resort instrument of state policy, any state worth its name should know how to use them effectively. Since military is also a double edged sword, they also need to learn to use them without hurting themselves. Some of the suggested measures to lower the risk or threat threshold are:

a. Maintain lean and professionalised armed forces to meet legitimate defence requirements of the state. Do not permit armed forces to indulge in empire building. (this tendency is discussed in militarism.)

b. Impart political education without politicising them. Constitutional basis of the relationship and their allegiance to the Constitution must be driven home.

c. Keep service conditions of soldiers good without pampering them. Dissatisfied soldiers may seek redressal of their grievances in an unacceptable and unorthodox manner.

d. Extend recruitment/selection to the armed forces to all strata of society without reservation or allocation. Military of a democratic nation must be nationally representative in character.

The above writing is an analytical description of praetorianism as a phenomenon in the politico-military domain. Use of certain terms and expressions should not be construed as condemnation or recommendatory of the phenomenon. Whether it is malady or remedy is conditional. When political system and constitution in vogue enjoy public approbation and also the system is working satisfactorily, military usurping political power would be a malady. On the other hand if the country is saddled with corrupt, dictatorial, malevolent or non-functional government much against the will of the people but they can not throw off the yoke, then military intervention may be remedy. Military's subservience to such a political system makes them collaborators in crime. In either of the cases it is not a free game for the military. A conscientious soldier should consider the following aspects:

a. Legality of polity (constitutional validity of the rule including interpretation by judiciary and other independent/autonomous institutions/bodies).

b. In case of institutional deadlock, feasibility of resolving the deadlock militarily.

c. Possibility of national security being jeopardised during the process of intervention

d. Ends must justify resort to this special means.

Military is an important institution of democracy and its representatives in the politico-military domain are responsible senior officers who can not be guided by rule of thumb. They have to make the final choice taking into consideration the law of the land, dictates of their conscience and orders of their political masters. They are required to function in the highest interests of the state. In the event of any interference, the aim should be to facilitate return to the constitutional ways within the shortest possible time frame. At no time should the soldier aspire to abrogate or suspend the Constitution for a long time. While intervening to resolve any institutional deadlock, the soldier must conduct himself in a non-partisan manner.

Militarism

'Militarism' is often misused term, although the

dictionary does not list any secondary meaning or usage. It is probably, proximity and resemblance of the term to words militant (adjective) and militate (verb) that mislead people. A book about non-occurence of military coup in India by Apurba Kundu bears the title 'Militarism in India - The Civil Society in Consensus'. An Indian journalist Anuradha M Chenoy in her article 'Muscular Militarism' extends the phenomenon to familial, societal and even gender relations. In both instances glaring misuse of the term is also a case of letting imagination run amok. In this writing the term 'militarism' is used and is to be understood in accordance with lexicon meaning. It is treated as a malady in politico-military domain but conditionally.

Obligation of a political community (state) to maintain armed forces is an incontrovertible premise propounded by Professor Michael Howard and has been quoted earlier in this chapter. The state meets its obligation keeping in mind her legitimate defence requirements and also other available options. However, the expression 'legitimate defence requirements' does not render itself in absolute terms. For instance, the tiny state of Israel maintains an aggresive military posture due to existential threat but pronouncement of Ms Condeleezzaa Rice, National Security Advisor to former President George Bush that America faces existential threat to its security sounds rather exaggerated. Militarism as advocacy of aggressive use of military power is an attitude (state policy) but actual build up and use of force is a physical demonstration. Such a political philosophy (militarism) may not care to exhaust other available options or instruments like diplomatic or economic.

The armed forces in the hands of such a political community are instruments of instant use instead of last resort. They assert their right to pre-emptive action and action without restraint.

This operational methodology is wedded to the politics of unilateralism and hegemony. Fortunately for the mankind, United States of America is the only country in the comity of nations, whose National Security Policy permits extreme militarism of this kind. Other western nations who do intervene, do so under the aegis of the world body.

There is also the need to consider the physical demonstration of the phenomenon as it has profound impact on other vital national activities like economy, diplomacy, industrialisation and finally military establishment itself. Military consumes vast quantity of material and financial resources, employs large manpower both directly and indirectly and provides stimulus to industry, yet has no tangible productivity. At best its existence promotes an environment of security where other nation building activities flourish. A nation's spending on military (including research and development) is significant. Any large scale imbalance in spending can upset or ruin national economy. Defence related industry, both in public and private sector tend to form a lobby to influence governmental decision on military spending. The lobbies are inhabited by a large number of ex-servicemen.

Possession of 'credible level' of force leads to display and deployment of such hardware. It is usual for countries to display their military prowess at independence day or republic day parades and on other national occasions. New acquisitions or achievements in indigenous research and development are also proudly displayed. The other kind of display, bordering on aggressive posturing is conduct of large scale military exercises in areas close to adversary's territory. Such chest thumping or sabre rattling displays are detrimental to promotion of friendly or good neighbourly relations. On the contrary such displays can undo whatever diplomacy may have achieved. At times it may prompt similar retaliatory gestures from the adversary.

For instance the Indian exercise "Brasstacks" prompted Pakistan to conduct "Zarb-e-Momin".

Militarism affects military establishment itself in strange ways. Acquisition, display and operation of military hardware become a hobby horse with some senior soldiers so much so that force building turns into empire building. The limits of rational legitimate defence requirements are grossly transgressed. The ambitious soldier then transfers his military prowess to political arena. Beginning with gradual and slow meddling in domestic politics, he elevates himself to the position of arbiter of political power.

Politicisation of armed forces

"I do not want politics to enter the Services," which will be the result if these men (Indian National Army) are reinstated. The day politics enters the army, it will be a sad day".

- Paraphrased response of Jawaharlal Nehru

'Soldier, Scholar and Statesman' was often a tribute to the multifaceted persona of yesteryears, particularly during medieval times. In our times and changed circumstances, polity and military have evolved as distinct professionalised domains. They are also important institutions of the state with attendant responsibilities. Therefore, any individual who attempts to merge these distinct spheres of activity is viewed with sceptism rather than admiration.

Despite the caution exercised by Nehru to insulate the armed forces from politicisation, his protege and Defence Minister Krishna Menon was guilty of favouritism, violation of established norms and consequently politicisation of armed forces. What motives drive soldiers and politicians into this unholy alliance? The near correct answer is that the unbridled ambition of the soldiers and avarice and ignorance of the politicians make them collaborators in this despicable conduct. The pyramidical organisational structure of the armed forces and intense competition can frustrate the career aspirations and ambitions of its soldiers. Some soldiers may seek political patronage. There are others who seek post-retirement offers like gubernatorial posts, ambassadorship and chairmanship of public sector undertakings. Members of the polity have their own reasons too. Indian polity is by and large ignorant of matters military. They tend to seek information, opinion and guidance from senior soldiers to overcome their handicap. It is a well known fact that procurement of defence equipment involves massive spending. Some avaricious politicians may seek to enrich themselves or fill their party coffers in the process. Senior soldiers may oblige them with favourable response on reciprocal basis.

Just as rapid building of force levels is not militarism, a soldier nurturing political ambitions in his post retirement life is not a violator. The state may benefit as they transfer their expertise and experience to other domains. In fact that was the spirit of the recommendations of Sarkaria Commission. It is the process, circumstances and motivation under which soldiers hitch on to the political band wagon that should be considered while determining the desirability of transgression. During the 1991 Lok Sabha elections, a large number of senior retired defence officers joined political parties. The phenomenon was unprecedented. The Ex-servicemen League too appealed to the electorate to favour a particular political party, ostensibly to seek redressal of long standing grievances. This sudden rush of political consciousness among the supposedly apolitical soldiers does indicate that something had gone amiss. The fact that nothing came of it is a poor consolation.

While the suppliant soldiers are obliging to their political patrons, the disgruntled and rebellious may seek patronage of opposing political parties. Some have in the past joined with forces who openly profess secessionist aspirations. These self-seeking soldiers can cause great harm to the morale and security of armed forces and other institutions of democracy.

Armed forces are not a political constituency and it is in society's interest that they are left to maintain their apolitical attitude.

Interservice rivalry

"Chief of Defence Staff is a good idea but it should be introduced after my tenure"

- A Chief of Staff

Inter service rivalry is an old malady that afflicts most armed forces but needs to be resolutely settled when it turns dysfunctional adversely affecting operational efficacy. In our country despite the asymmetry of size, the three service chiefs who represent their respective services are placed at par in the politico-military domain. Their enthusiasm to advance the interests of their own service in matters like sub allocation of defence budget or procurement of hardware often triggers intense rivalry. For instance, Army and Navy may regard integral air power as necessary for operational efficacy but Air Force may percieve it as loss of legitimate role. Appointment of Chief of Defence Staff (CDS) has not fructified till now due to an air of mutual suspicion amongst the services. Polity and bureaucracy have vested interests and apprehensions not to facilitate the process. Such a situation is not conducive for effective conduct of joint operations which is very necessary in present day warfare.

Corruption in arms procurement

Indigenisation of Indian armed forces is a distant dream because India not only missed industrial revolution but has also demonstrated socio-cultural inability to quickly absorb technology. It is, therefore, inevitable for India to resort to acquisition of military hardware from foreign sources. The acquisition process involves multiple agencies, large financial budget and protracted time frames thus rendering it vulnerable to corruption. A procedural methodology called offsets which was meant to facilitate transfer of technology along with hardware has grown into full fledged industry by itself. Despite well stipulated procedures, the unrelated offsets facilitate corruption rather than transfer of technology. Therefore, the only safeguard against corruption in procurement of defence hardware is honesty and integrity of individuals who tread the domain.

Chapter-2

Resume of politico-military relations in India

"No civilisation was so little equipped to cope with the outside world; no country was so easily raided and plundered' and learned so little from its disasters."

- V S Naipaul in his book
'India- A wounded civilisation'.

Sweeping deprecation of India's gross neglect of her territorial security by V.S. Naipaul may sound uncharitable and hurt nationalistic pride, but nevertheless it is a historical truism. A feeble protest to that observation could be that civilisation is too general geographically and it is the political communities (nation's states) with well demarcated territorial boundaries that clash with each other (the words civilisation and country have been used interchangeably in the quote). India acquired neither nationalistic character nor geographical configuration resembling its present day reality until late nineteenth century. However, it is unfortunate that complacent neglect of national security has continued even in modern India as borne out by the events in post independence period. Lack of strategic thinking, ill prepared (equipped) armed forces and unsatisfactory higher direction of defence are easily discernible. Yet, the Indian polity through its ostrich like attitude has all along refused to squarely face these vital issues of national security. India's total neglect of lessons of history is not easily comprehensible. Is it due to Hindu complacence or Gandhian pacifism or Nehruvian diplomatic idealism or political ignorance or bureaucratic malevolence or combination of all these?

We need to revisit history to determine the extent to which unsatisfactory or sub optimal politico military relations have precipitated apathetic attitude towards national security issues. For obvious reasons the review must commence from the time polity and military segregated or emerged as two distinct specialised professional institutions. In the Indian context evolution of all important institutions has been influenced by her colonial past. Both polity and military existed in some form even before independence. While it would not be grossly incorrect to date the coming into being of 'polity' with nationalistic conscience or character as late nineteenth century, there are regiments in the Indian army which are much older than that. The military establishment in India long preceded polity and struck deep roots to develop their foundational basis, value systems and attitudes. Yet, it was not a straight case of putting cart before the horse, instead it was both institutions evolving simultaneously but under significantly different circumstances, only to be yoked together after independence. Lack of mutuality of purpose and antipathy born out of different operating modes (non-violence vis-a-vis armed force) did distance polity and military in pre independence India. Any retrospection can not be chronologically rigid or accurate. The purpose of this review is to facilitate understanding of development of inter institutional relations. The resume has been divided into three parts - pre independence era, independent India and other events of special significance.

Pre independence era

> *"A society may attain independence through non-violent means, yet possession of armed force is an essential obligation of any political community (country) to safeguard that independence.*
>
> **- Author**

Although anomalies in the politico-military relations (domain) in India are attributable to circumstances of genesis of these two institutions, other differences have accentuated them. During the pre independence period, the polity (if it can be called so) consisted of loosely knit cohesion of nationalist leaders under the domineering influence of Gandhian non-violence as their guiding political philosophy. Gandhi-Nehru duo succeeded in forcing militant leader Subhas Chandra Bose out of Congress and into political wilderness in 1939.

Their (polity) knowledge of body military and national security were rather vague. This vague awareness caused two major issues of concern namely, excessive cost of maintaining a standing army and opening up of opportunities to the higher echelons in the army to Indians. In this context, achievements of Indian Sandhurst Committee and Defence Sub committee were so significant that the intake of Indians to Royal Military College Sandhurst was doubled in due course.

During this period (pre independence) the armed forces were functioning in service of the imperial power. The colonial masters (British) fully exploited the vast manpower resources of Indian sub continent to build up their military establishment both to perpetuate their rule and for their war effort. There was mass recruitment for below officers' rank from select communities classified as 'martial classes'. Entry to the officers' cadre was opened to Indians later in restricted number and selectively. The British authorities kept the army cocooned from political influence by administrative measures that made their life protected and comfortable.The nationalist leaders too did not favour exploiting the army as a political instrument for freedom movement. Due to the insulation of the British administrative measures and exercise of restraint by the polity, the military remained unpoliticised. The apolitical conduct of the Indian armed forces in the post independence era may be regarded as continuation of that tradition.

When faced with ambiguity about their loyalty to the government vis-a-vis higher cause of national movement, the army sought clarification and the lurking doubt about the basis of their loyalty and its purpose was settled through dialogue with polity as demonstrated in Excerpt I.

The then military officers of Indian origin although relatively junior, clearly understood the basis of loyalty as to the legitimate government of the day and not to any other emotional appeal and they adhered to it. It is noteworthy that both polity and military stood their ground well when faced with the question of reinduction of erstwhile members of the Indian National Army.

Excerpt I - Dialogue between Polity and Military

	Motilal Nehru and Lieutenant Thimayya
M.Nehru	We are going to win independence. Perhaps not this year or the next, but sooner or later the British will be driven out. When this happens, India will stand alone. We will have no one to protect us but ourselves. It is then that our survival will depend on men like you.
Thimayya	You mean that we should stay with the army to learn as much as we can?
M. Nehru	Exactly
	Lala Lajpat Rai and Lieutenant Thorat
Thorat	Sir, do you think that we have done wrong in joining the Indian army, on the strength of which the British are ruling us?
LL Rai	No, I don't think so at all. How long will the British continue to rule us? Due day India shall become a free country and then we will need trained men like you. So work hard and prepare yourself for that moment.

While political (apolitical) correctness of the military was praiseworthy, they did not display same level of maturity on matters of personal ethical code of conduct. Their frivolous attitude is amply revealed in two reminiscences placed at Excerpt II.

In absence of national identity and ethos in preindependent India, the armed forces adopted two dominant thoughts namely, rigid regimental spirit and the concept of "officer and gentleman'. The former developed a blinkered vision and the latter was not amenable to precise definition. Much depended on the maturity and inclination of the individual. Some anglomaniac Brindian (borrowed expression) officers went overboard and adopted dandy life behaviour, which was neither enviable nor sustainable in independent India. This attitude distanced them from troops as they did not make any attempt to identify themselves with troops.

Another attitudinal aspect of pre independence era which has shaped politico-military relations in modern India (post independence) is the polity's perceptions of roles for military. Two differing views of nationalist leaders are placed at Excerpt III.

Excerpt II - Code of Coduct

General J N Chauduri's recollection of code of conduct of Indian Gentleman cadets at Sandhurst

Indian GCs developed their own unwritten code of conduct, a break from which it would have meant ostracism. The rules were fairly simple. An Indian GC was to tip his servant 5 shillings weekly, which was double the normal rate. At cinema, the Indian GCs were to use the more expensive balcony seats and not the cheaper stalls. Visiting 'Ma Hart', the RMC's favourite pawn shop was taboo. Attendance at the end of term ball, a very colourful, affair, was forbidden unless one could bring an Indian girl to it. Finally, cutting in on or filching another Indian GC's girlfriend was the greatest crime of all. I suppose the first three rules were designed to show that Indians were not a poor race. Rule 4 made sense and rule 5, looking at the shortage of girls who in those days would be seen with Indians, was a safety device.

General BM Kaul's reflection on the training at Sandhurst

I had imbibed much at Sandhurst. I learnt a code of conduct, a sense of discipline and the significance of honour. I was taught a set of principles true to spiritual values by which can be judged what is right. I acquired the rudiments of military knowledge, the basic techniques of my profession and to appreciate the importance of turnout and skill at professional work and games and also to face agreeable and unpleasant situations alike. I was taught how to play the game, to know what the qualities of leadership were, the sense of many values and the honour of serving one's country selflessly and with devotion.

While Nehru's views and attitude may be regarded as rational if not appropriate; Gandhi's role prescription for the armed forces displays ignorance of national security. There are national politico-military models where the armed forces are employed for nation building activities but suggestions to use them as handmaiden for social service are downright ridiculous. At this point certain observations on Gandhi are apt and in place. He was at best a social reformer but as was his wont, he would meddle with affairs on which he was quite ill informed or ignorant. It is dreadful to conceive of India as a nation state, had we subscribed to his whims and ideas in areas like economy, industrialisation, education and national security.

Excerpt III - Polity's Role Perception of Military

> **Jawaharlal Nehru in *Young India* 01 Oct 1931**
>
> "Our present (1931) army is efficient, we must bear in mind that we shall have to re-organise it completely and create out of it and out of fresh material a truly national army,with a national purpose and a national outlook."
>
> **MK Gandhi in *Harijan* 21 Apr 1946**
>
> "Soldiers should plough the land, dig wells, clean latrines, and do every other constructive work that they can, and thus turn the people's hatred of them into love. While the good will of the whole world is good enough for defence of the country."

The state of politico-military relations in pre-independence period may be summarised as follows:

- The polity (then comprising of nationalist leaders) was blissfully unaware of the fact that maintenance of armed forces is an essential obligation of sovereignty. The polity also lacked competence in the use of a powerful instrument as military.
- The nationalist leaders were innocent idealists who hoped that military would have no role in the emerging comity of nations in post colonial period. They also had great faith in new

international institutions like United Nations Organisation and Non-aligned Movement.

- There was no mutuality of purpose between polity and military. It also resulted in lack of interactive interface between the two.

Post independence period

> *"The armed forces eked out their existence ------------- like a neglected wife. She was there, her presence was comforting, on occasions even useful---------but essentially governmental policy did not prescribe any definitive objective for their services"*
>
> **PVR Rao**
> **- A former defence secretary**

> *"Attitude of political leadership towards the armed forces in the first decade of independence was very much like that of a teetotaler who had inherited a brewery"*
>
> **-A retired Air Marshal**
> **responding to questionnaire by Apurba Kundu**

Nascent nation states need to pay as much attention to building important institutions and their working relations as to other nation building endeavours like economy, techno-industrial infrastructure and human development. Building politico-military relations is particularly important if the country has opted for democratic norms of governance. Countries emerging out of colonial rule do inherit some institutions and organisations but they were usually designed to suit administrative needs of colonial masters. However, restructuring the state apparatus utilising the remnant of the colonial past but to suit the new political ethos of the state is a practical solution. India on independence inherited the military establishment deeply entrenched in the colonial past. There was not even a modicum of rapport between bodies polity and military due to the then prevalent situation summarised in the previous paragraph.

Therefore, at the dawn of Indian independence ignorant polity (lacking in military related knowledge) and complacent cantonment military found themselves yoked together in a mutually indifferent alliance compelled by constitutional obligations. The much needed functional interface was provided by the malovalent bureaucracy playing interlocutory role.

The quick succession of events in the early part of post independence era provided no respite for rationalisation of these relations. Instead some of the events further accentuated the strained relations and the attitude changed from mutual indifference to disdain for each other. However, the military was at the receiving end due to constitutional status. Some important events after 1947 that influenced or were influenced by the politico-military relations have been grouped together under separate heads based on issues involved.

Higher direction of defence (War)

> *"The statesman who seeing war inevitable; fails to strike first is guilty of a crime against his country"*
>
> **- Von Der Goltz; German strategist**

India's first Prime Minister Jawaharlal Nehru upset the applecart of politico-military relations by relegating the armed forces to the level of neglect. While his vision and genuine concern for other nation building activities were admirable, his neglect of the armed forces was deplorable. He was over confident of himself as a statesman to the extent of being arrogant. The most visible demonstration of his attitude was reflected in his choice of defence ministers. The first one, Sardar Baldev Singh was in the cabinet as a compromise sikh candidate rather than for his knowledge of matters military. During this period, differences between bureaucrat HM Patel who ran the ministry and Gen Cariappa are too familiar. The next Gopalaswamy Ayyangar, respected by the military, died in office after ten months. Nehru himself held the charge for the next two years but delegated the functional responsibility to a junior minister. The next defence minister Kailash Nath Katju was no better equipped for the job.

The most important functional purpose of maintaining politico-military relations at optimal level is to facilitate better conduct of operations. The make shift arrangements of politico-military relations was put to test in the immediate aftermath of independence. Faced with aggression by Razaakars and Pakistani troops in Kashmir, Nehru opted for unilateral ceasefire and rushed to the United Nations much against the advice of the military but to meet 'higher requirements of international peace'. It resulted in creation of 'Pakistan Occupied Kashmir' (POK) albeit loss of territory to India.

The Chinese debacle of 1962 was no bolt out of the blue as flooding of Himalayan rivers. Nehru chose to turn a Nelson's eye to the border incursions by Chinese and was preoccupied building his own image as an international statesman. He was actively engaged in preaching his 'panchsheel' and proclaiming 'Hindi Chini bhai bhai'. In the meantime army was left ill-equipped, untrained and without any tangible deployment plans. Tha political apparatus for higher direction of war consisted of Prime Minister Nehru and his irascible Defence Minister Krishna Menon. The latter was also responsible for politicising the army by favourtism and violation of norms. The concept of collective responsibility of cabinet was never put into practice on an important aspect like national security. Thus a simmering border dispute was allowed to snowball into a debacle. The callous attitude of the government to matters of national security is reflected in their lack of attention till as late as 22nd September 1962. Nehru (PM) was in London, Krishna Menon (DM) was in New York to attend UN Security Council session, Morarji Desai (FM) was in Washington DC and Lal Bahadur Shastri (HM) was in Kerala. The higher direction of war was left to Joint Secretary (Defence) Harish C. Sarin who signed the executive order to evict the Chinese. Pushing an ill-equipped and unprepared army into war; humiliating defeat and loss of territory are all part of Indian Military history. There is no ambiguity about the attributability of blame.

The 1965 Indo-Pak War ended in a draw and the then Prime Minister Lal Bahadur Shastri signed the Tashkent agreement under Russian mediation. In the aftermath of war, strategically important Haji Pir Pass and the large areas of occupied territory were returned to Pakistan. Political communities (states) usually resort to war after diplomacy has failed; but diplomacy nullifying the military gains without strong compulsions is rare in inter-state conflicts. It may be regarded as lack of mutuality of purpose between polity and military. It definitely is poor statecraft.

In 1971 Indo-Pak War, often referred to as Liberation of Bangladesh constitutes a watershed in many respects. Apart from culminating in a spectacular and decisive victory for India, there are other noteworthy aspects.

a. In early 1971 when the Prime Minister suggested armed intervention to resolve refugee problem, then Chief of Army Staff General Sam Manekshaw asked for nine months preparatory time. Indira Gandhi conceded to his request. While the General was busy preparing and acquiring necessary hardware, the Prime Minister was engaged in building favourable international opinion. This was the first politico-military collaborative effort in independent India.

b. The war changed the political geography of the sub-continent – a new nation (Bangladesh) was born thus eliminating for ever two front threat from Pakistan. Whether it was a deliberate master stroke of strategy or a mere coincidence is open to speculation.

c. In its repeat performance, the government of India did not link the release of 93,000 prisoners of war to negotiate the border dispute on the western front.

d. The inter service cooperation (Navy and Air Force) was so poor that Air Force lost maritime reconnaissance role to the Indian Navy.

In 1987, the then Prime Minister Rajiv Gandhi sought to become a peacemaker between LTTE (an ethnic Tamil militant group) and Sri Lankan armed forces. Whether it was strategic assertion or compulsion of domestic politics, it definitely was unsound method of using a powerful instrument of state policy like the armed forces. Stuck between an un friendly host country and violent militancy, the Indian army suffered more casualities than in any other war since independence. There was no positive political outcome. Even the initiator of the peace process paid with his life. Sri Lankan operations are often referred to as India's Vietnam.

The Kargil War of 1999 was fought on Indian territory and therefore victory did not result in any territrorial gains. It was sheer repulsing an incursion. Yet, there were some noteworthy features. It is to the credit of the BJP government that the Kargil Review Committee report was tabled in parliament and made public. This was in stark contrast to the Henderson Brooks Committee report which remains unpublicised even after sixty years. This show of transparency by government was an achievement in itself. The inter-service cooperation (Air-land war) was unsatisfactory to the level of total disappointment. Till date coordinated defence management is absent except for some cosmetic changes.

Civil military interface

After India's political independence, the Indian armed forces were quick to appreciate their changed status and role as an important institution of the Indian democracy. They gracefully accepted civil supremacy of rule as a functional mode as compared to militaries of many other political communities in similar circumstances. Yet, there were occasions when the enviable amity in the politico-military domain was vitiated by mutual suspicion and at times confrontational posturing for which both institutions share the blame.

The praetorian ghost has raised its ugly head on more than one occasion to haunt the insecure mind of the Indian polity. Ridiculous suggestion by the then Brigadier KM Cariappa for the military to assume political power after independence was viewed with suspicion. He was suspected of nurturing political ambition. His act probably earned him an ambassadorial (high commissioner) assignment to New Zealand. Flamboyance of Field Marshall Manekshaw made him a suspect, but plain talking between him and Indira Gandhi set the fears at rest. Recently, the media unaware of the norms and regulations interpreted minor movements of troops in the vicinity of national capital as veiled challenge of authority by Gen VK Singh.

Feeble resistance of General KS Thimayya to politicisation and interference in the internal administration of the army by Krishna Menon was bulldozed by Nehru. In a similar reenactment by George Fernandes, Admiral Vishnu Bhagwat became the first service chief to be sacked. Although both defence ministers are often put in the same league as notoriously abrasive, the conduct of both service chiefs was none too bold or commendable.

Even at other times, as ignoramus defence ministers

preferred to function through bureaucracy and depended heavily on them, the services were in effect subordinated even to the bureaucracy. Thus supremacy of civil rule was established in a ham handed way.

The other serious malady that afflicts this domain is corruption. High value defence hardware acquisitions are seen by some members of the polity as opportunities to enrich themselves and also fill the party coffers. It is possible that some members of the uniformed fraternity too received some fringe benefits. The first instance of corruption was purchase of jeeps where involvement of Krishna Menon was suspected. Cases of corruption in the 60's were overshadowed by imminent threat of war. When Rajiv Gandhi was the Prime Minister (80's), Indian armed forces attempted major modernisation. During this period procurement of artillery gun (Bofors) and HDW submarines came under the cloud. There were instances of corruption reported during the BJP regime too. However, the politicians invariably escape personal culpability. Recently even some defence officers were involved in various scams like Adarsh and Sukhna land case.

How should the soldiers conduct themselves in such circumstances?

Senior soldiers treading the politico-military domain must stand their ground well even while maintaining constitutional propriety. They should steer clear of controversies and avoid media exposure but when compelled 'plain speaking' helps. Soldiers should advance themselves through professional competence and not through political patronage. It makes them proud soldiers and institutions stronger.

Having an individual who has understanding of military matters as the defence minister is useful. There are quite a few soldiers and bureaucrats who have hitched on to political band wagons after their retirement. Their service could be of help. If such persons enjoy no electoral prospects a way out can be found. Force planning and procurement are highly normative activities. It is in the interests of the institutions and the country that they remain so. Adhocism and arbitrariness fuel corruption and must be avoided.

Note: All the excerpts in this chapter have been culled out from 'Militarism in India' by Apurba Kundu.

Chapter-3

Higher direction of defence (war)

"There is always more spirit in attack than defence".

-Titus Livius

Quite frequently phrases 'Higher Direction of Defence' and 'Higher Direction of War' are used interchangeably although there is subtle distinction between the two. Considering the obsession of Indian polity with non-violence, non-agression, non-alignment and peaceful coexistence; it should come as a great relief that saints in the Indian polity do not insist on adopting Orwellian newspeak to call it 'Higher Direction of Peace'. Despite similar apparatus and functional methodology, the distinction between the two becomes apparent when the outcome of the two processes are considered. Working of the apparatus for Higher Direction of Defence culminates in defence policy which is a broad guideline for the build up of armed forces and developing strategic options. Higher Direction of War involves governmental decision making on conduct of operations, use of higher weapons of war and finally executive orders for the armed forces. However, what is common to both processes is that without professional inputs from the military the outcomes are bound to be disastrous.

These two processes are the highest level of functional interaction between the political executive and military. It is to be noted that President as the Supreme Commander is only the notional head to stress the autonomous status of the military as an institution of democracy. Defence Minister is the Chief Executive and the functional head of the armed forces. However in deference to the 'collective responsibility of the cabinet' enshrined in the Indian Constitution, he works under the overall supervision of the Prime Minister. In furtherance of the above objective, a system of committees and councils is adopted for management of higher defence. Political executive, often lacking in military related expertise (at most times even awareness) and to unburden itself introduces bureaucratic supervision in a high handed manner taking shelter under the constitutional provisions or rules made under it.

Higher direction of defence

Defence policy of a nation state is the confluence of will of the people, governmental decisions and military related expertise. Will of the people is heard in nation states which observe democratic norms and people enjoy unrestricted freedom of expression. However, the extent of its influence depends on public awareness of military matters, maturity level of democracy and efficacy of media as an institution of democracy. It finds expression in the form of parliamentary or public debates and protests or support expressed through media and physical demonstrations. In mature and sensitive democracies the public voice can influence election manifesto and government policies. The course of most American wars worldwide were decided by public opinion at home.

National security is a complex domain and has many facets and as expected is influenced by multiple factors. The armed forces provide the military related expertise in an advisory role. Government decision making process on the defence related issues is facilitated through a system of committees and councils. By design these are ideal structures or fora as they facilitate multi-disciplinary (holistic) approach to defence; are rooted in democratic norms; provide for hierarchial decision making and avoid ad-hocism or high handedness of individuals. Details of these structures or flowchart of decision making are not being elaborated upon in this writing as primary concern of this book is attitude and conduct of people functioning in this domain. The Indian experience with the system of committees and councils has been none too satisfactory as most of these are born either as crisis management outfits in the aftermath of a crisis. Some are still born and some are susceptible to infantile mortality.

Those that survive, waste away to extinction as

utility of these bodies depends on the whims and fancies of the polity. The reasons for such gross neglect are obvious. For Indian politicians national security is not an elecroral issue and defence policy is not a priority. An attempt can be made to optimise the functioning of these structures by tasking them on regular basis and established norms. These bodies must be staffed by mature and responsible individuals with clear perception of national security.

Higher Direction of Defence is essentially a planning activity which is dependent on intelligence (information) on various aspects political, economic, technology, war making capability of potential adversaries and also geo-political realities. Without accurate and reliable inputs the planning process will have to depend on intellegent guess work thus rendering the ensuing actions shot in the dark. Intelligence gathering and processing is carried out by multiple agencies under different ministries. An activity that should ideally be a cooperative venture, usually turns out to be undesirable rivalry between the agencies and ministries to claim credit or to disown responsibility for failures. In order to overcome such tendencies, the channels for transmission of intelligence and the speed should be specified for various contingencies.

Defence planning is an open ended protracted process because of certain compelling aspects like life of platforms (capital equipment); training requirement of personnel; lead time required for procurement (import) or production (indigenous) and large financial outlays that need to be spread across long time. On the other hand the process of long term planning is hassled by rapid obsolescence of equipment due to quantum jumps in technology and changing geo-political situation. There is no denying the fact that a protracted process tends to breed complacence bordering on neglect.

We bemoan the lack of 'strategic thought process' legacy, yet we have failed to make an earnest beginning since independence. Ideally defence planning should have been one of the focussed streams of nation building. It is important that political executive (government) articulates defence policy and national security doctrine in clear terms. Lack of clarity and practice of ad-hocism by the government encourages empire building dreams of chiefs of staff of armed forces. Ad-hoc demands by the services in terms of manpower lead to cost escalation and at times wasteful expenditure. It also increases probablity of corruption.

The above assertions about banes of poor planning and ad-hocism are validated by past events. For instance, there are several defence related agencies operating in the Indian maritime scenario like Indian Navy, Indian Coastguard, Customs and Marine wings of Police of coastal states. The Indian government added one more, in the aftermath of terrorist attack on Bombay. While the government is vociferously announcing its political philosophy of non-agression and non-hegemonistic designs, the Indian Navy is building multi-carrier power projection force at phenomenal cost. The Indian government has been trying since inependence to contain the size if not downsize the army. On its part, the Indian Army, the second largest in the world claims that it is understaffed and has aggresive growth plans. The Indian Air Force too, does not want to be left behind. Unscrupulous polity on their part views adhocism in matter of acquisition of capital platforms or equipment as an opportunity for corruption to either fill party coffers or their pockets. Soldiers who collude with them in this heinous act for personal gains betray their subordinates, service and the nation.

Having examined the process and the possibilities, it is only fit that we examine the mental and moral attributes of the soldiers functioning in this domain. In the ultimate analysis defence policy of a state is well informed decision based on evaluation of threat perceptions to national security or interests; possibility and the kind of military response and resources that can be allocated for the purpose. Military related expertise is only a component, though an important one. Effectiveness in the domain depends on one's ability to comprehend dynamics of foreign policy, compulsions of economics, demands of technology and much else. An ideal soldier in the domain may be described as 'scholar warrior'. The military establishment has a training system in place to equip its personnel at varying levels of responsibilities. But, what happens to the other participants in the domain, namely the indifferent polity and generalist bureaucracy?

Higher direction of war

The distinction between Higher Direction of Defence and Higher Direction of War based on the process outcomes has already been explained. The other crucial distinction is the timeframe involved. Modern conventional wars (as opposed to regular war) rarely last long. Further reaction times are much shorter. The advent of technology and nature of modern munitions of war make it so. Any apparatus (command structure) for Higher Direction of War should be capable of meeting this demand.

A brief recapitulation of the past wars India has fought is illuminating. During the India-China War of 1962, there was no key member of the cabinet present in India or New Delhi to direct the military.That crucial and inalienable task was left to bureaucracy by default. During the India-Pakistan War of 1971, even after months of notice and planning interservice cooperation was less than satisfactory. Indian intervention in Sri Lanka was near disaster. Even during the Kargil operations (fought inside Indian territory) close air support to the army was available only intermittently.

Not withstanding the final outcome of the above mentioned wars, it is evident that all is not well with Indian attitude and approach to national security. In a modern conventional war mere possession of numerical or material superiority may not ensure success even when the adversary is a smaller or an equal country. In a nuclear scenario it could be disastrous. A credible organisational structure for Higher Direction of War (HDW) is an imperative to meet the challenges of modern warfare. Such dynamic organisational structure should be able to provide the following:

a. A single point reference on defence matters and conduct of operations

b. Clear and unambiguous protocol for devolution of responsibility/command in the politico-military domain

c. Minimise reaction time and capacity for conduct of joint warfare.

d. Capacity for directing strategic (nuclear) forces.

All these qualitative stipulations of the mechanism for HDW can be met by institutionalising Chief of Defence Staff (CDS). However, this rational proposal has been moved to back burner due to unfounded, frivolous and selfish reservations from all parties concerned. Therefore, it is prudent that proposal of modalities for institutionalising CDS begin with objection handling.

Indian polity haunted by the praetorian ghost regards CDS too powerful an institution which can threaten democratic norms. The bureaucracy which regard governance as their exclusive prerogative would not like the proposal to fructify. Navy and Air Force have apprehensions that due to its sheer size, the Army as a dominant service would receive favourable consideration in matters of appointment and budgetary allocations. Two sister services should accept geo-political reality rather than seeking false parity with Army. These apprehensions and reservations have found an alibi in legal domain. Government of India Transaction of business and Allocation of business rules 1961 derived under article 77 (3) of Constitution stipulate the methodology for governance wherein the bureaucracy acts as intermediary between polity and military.

CDS has to be a senior defence officer with knowledge and acumen in matters military. A retired individual is preferable so that inter service rivalry is toned down to the extent possible and also facilitate integration of the institution into Ministry of Defence (political executive). Such an individual can be nominated to Rajya Sabha (Upper House) as it is unlikely that he enjoys any electoral prospects. His tenure could coincide with his membership of the Upper House which will give continuity in office which is essential for long term defence planning. Ranking him as minister of state under the defence minister would establish him in the politico-military domain. Whole range of defence related activities like defence policy, research and development and production may be brought under his purview. Neither the CDS nor the chiefs of staff would have any force levels under their direct command. Thus the shortcoming of the present system—the chiefs of staff are present where not required and are absent where required, would also be resolved. The proposals may necessitate amendments to the Constitution and the rules derived from it. The sanctity of the Constitution pales into a workable via media when it is an issue of paramount importance like national security.

Supremacy of civil rule in a democracy is a political ideal but the rectitude of members of polity and bureaucracy who tread the politico-military domain is not axiomatic. There have been instances where prime minister or defence minister have misled the parliament, indulged in unethical practices and humiliated the soldiers. Submissiveness of soldiers under such circumstances will make them bolder. The soldiers in this domain must take firm stand where required and be ready to face the consequences. It is recommended that they seek involvement of other important institutions and offices of democracy. Leaders do not search for precedents, they create one if necessary.

It is ardently hoped that indoctrination of soldiers on ethical norms will inculcate the moral attributes. Their moralistic stance and firmness will deter the illegitimate conduct of others in the domain. Combat related issues to be dealt by the senior soldiers are discussed in Combat Philosophy.

Aid to civil power

The three armed forces collectively possess a wide range of specialisations and expertise. They can undertake almost any task. Their large number and organisational and material resources at their disposal enable them to assist civil authorities in times of natural calamities and man made disasters. The armed forces do not begrudge such demands. However, suggestions from some quarters that since they are instrument in the hands of government, they should be employed for other nation building activities is ridiculous. The armed forces are a specialised instrument and one must know how to use them.

Cantonment soldiering may not be possible in an evolved democracy but employing them for sundry purposes will dull the edge of husbandry with serious repercussions. In any case they need lot of time for training and maintenance of their equipment.

Chapter-4

Military and Media

"In the middle ages, armies carried their prostitutes. In the Iraq war, American and British armies are accompanied by journalists. This is presstitution"

- Uri Avnery
Israeli journalist

The homologous analogy in the above quote reflects the paradigm shift in inter-institutional relations. Whereas interactive and at times cooperative interface between military and media would have been far fetched and unimaginable in the pre world war era, the twentyfirst century is grappling with the idea of military embedded media. This transformation has been engendered by proliferation of egalitarian political idealogies and quantum jumps in media related technologies.

A brief survey of these tranformational changes provides an useful backdrop in understanding professional ethics and responsibilities of both soldiers and journalists. It will also help the military establishment to develop an effective media management strategy.

In authoritarian regimes the media is usually state owned or controlled and used as an instrument of state propoganda. Such stranglehold over media has now become almost impossible due to technological developments, particularly in relation to electronic media. In the newly emerged democracies after decolonisation, the media enjoyed greater freedom but the print media was owned by a few individuals who often displayed political leanings and were vulnerable to manipulation - the degree of manipulation varied from cajoling to coercion. Today in the evolved democracies, media enjoys unrestricted freedom. However, media has always been largely 'unorganised sector' despite presence of some statutory mechanisms and institutions. The concept of responsibility of media and professional code of conduct for the practitioners are evolving gradually. Media does not enjoy any constitutional or legal powers to correct or coerce other erring institutions in a democracy. In fact when it comes to reporting on military matters the Official Secrets Act has a smothering effect on media. Just as media evolved to gain greater freedom in new democratic societies, the military too became a public institution open to scrutiny. However, due to limited public awareness about military matters, probity about that institution grew only through episodes of commission and omission. Despite these handicaps media has emerged as powerful institution as it can mobilise public opinion in an overwhelming manner to bring about societal transformation.

While the media strives to inform analyse and educate the citizens about military matters, it behoves on the citizens to envince interest in these matters because the essence of egalitarian governance (democracy) is affirmative action by the citizens in the form of informed decision making, be it electoral process or other fora. The military matters are important to citizens because

- Functional domain of military is national security which is important to all.
- Military consumes significant share of national resources and has profound effects on aspects of national economy.
- Maladies in politico-military domain can have serious repurcussions on governance.

The Important need for the military to manage domestic and international public opinion in times of war is borne out by the fact that course of most of America's wars were to a great extent influenced by domestic opinion. In case of medium or small countries, adverse international opinion could attract intervention or sanctions that could cripple economic activity or military effort. During peace time military acts as an instrument of diplomacy. Domestic opinion affects budgetary allocation, force planning, civil-military relations and its own personnel policies.

In the trinity of military, media and people there is tug of war of sorts because of apparent conflicting requirements. Imperative of military to manage media relations, observance of professional rectitude by the media and the prerogative of the people to know can all be reconciled to build working interfaces. That brings us to the necessity to train media personnel in military related knowledge. Unfortunately defence journalism is not a formal course of study in most institutions/universities. It is, therefore, essentially an on job training. The life of a war correspondent reporting from ground zero is dangerous as that of any unarmed civilian in combat zone. Reporting conflict accurately and honestly entails that risk. However, there are embedded journalists who compromise on their professional ethics in exchange for their own safety, easy access to information and comfort. Restrictions on reporting due to risk of disclosing operational intelligence may be justified but distortion or propagandist journalism are not. In peace time, press briefings, there is a tendency among the media to accept handouts or statements by military as authentic after having enjoyed their hospitality.

Visual media harnessing the state of art media related technologies has emerged as a powerful instrument of moulding public opinion on military matter and consequently influencing public policy. This powerful instrument is also vulnerable to misuse by both journalists and soldiers (military) to serve the public with morphed information. Heart rending visuals of a burning young girl (victim of Napalm bomb) in Vietnam war and disgusting human desparity in the ill treatment of prisoners of war in Abu Ghraib camp were powerful enough to be moral compulsions on a government like that of United States. These were the genuine visuals of wartime atrocities. The US military morphed a rescue mission in Iraq to manage a favourable domestic opinion. In the build up to the Afghanistan War some inventive journalists were morphing visuals (complete with gunfire sound) from the roof tops of hotels in Peshawar and Islamabad.

There are occasions when media plays important roles, much beyond their legitimate duty of informing and moulding public opinion. During the first Gulf War, a news channel was instrumental in negotiating the surrender as there was no direct channel of communication between the adversaries. Visual media can provide clinching evidence in war crimes tribunals to bring errant soldiers to books. Video based sting operations have been useful in exposing corruption in defence procurement process.

The purpose of the above narration and deliberations is to deduce an ethical code of conduct both by the journalists and the soldiers in the process of media management. The journalists should avoid adopting extreme stance in relation to military. They are neither adversaries or collaborators and should therefore strive to maintain objectivity while reporting. Journalistic rules of professionalism and ethical code of conduct are continuously evolving and the choice of the right one depends on the sanity of the journalist. As for the soldiers, if their conduct during peacetime or combat roles has been dignified, there is no necessity for morphing. In fact transparency is advisable.

Chapter-5

Military Jurisprudence

Many nascent nations emerging out of colonial rule in post world war period adopted democratic norms of governance but experienced traumatic politico-military relations. Military establishments enjoyed an elevated status during the colonial rule but were subordinated to polity in the new democratic framework. The discontent with the altered relationship at times manifested in military seizing political power. The Indian armed forces gracefully accepted supremacy of civil rule as the essence of democracy and their apolitical stance throughout post independence period has been one of mature inter institutional relations. Even during emergency declared by Indira Gandhi, the military stood their ground well. On that count alone, the Indian experiment with democracy may be regarded as satisfactory. Due to this satisfactory state of inter institutional relations, the judiciary has never been called in or prompted to act as arbiter between polity and military. Therefore, contacts between the bodies military and judiciary have been only to redress grievances of individuals (both high ranking and junior level individuals). On some occasions when senior soldiers sought redressal of their grievances, the media which failed to recognise the subtle distinction, presented the cases as interinstitutional tussle/ challenge. There is also the need to understand military jurisprudence.

However, during the process of redressal (judgement) the judiciary has on occasions commented on the archaic jurisprudence in the Indian armed forces. Some Chiefs of Staff have lamented on the increase in the number of personnel seeking redressal of their grievances in civil courts. Sporadic incidents of insubordination, mutinous behaviour, fragging and deterioration of officer-man relationship have also occurred. All these incidents are directly or indirectly; intimately or remotely related to jurisprudence. Whatever is amiss in this domain of military jurisprudence and inter institutional relations is the concern of this writing. There is an anecdote of a young army officer, who having bet with his friends, streaked through a *baraat* (wedding procession) in a northern cantonment city. The officer was later identified and summarily awarded minor punishment for non-observance of anti malaria precautions. On the other hand personnel have either been court martialled or sent for psychiatric treatment for questioning illegitimate orders of superiors. Therefore, jurisprudence in the armed forces may widely vary from benevolent kangaroo court to malevolent tyranny.

Military establishments the world over characteristically resist change and such resistance is far greater in conservative societies. They often mistake stagnation for stability and archaic for tradition without realising that the only stability possible in our ever changing society is stability in motion. It is desirable that service conditions of personnel are in tune with contemporary socio-political environment as the armed forces have joined the main stream of society and no longer practice cantonment soldiering. Yet changes do not come about easily. For instance, in Britain a subject and employee of the crown could not sue the government, making it almost impossible to seek redressal of individual grievances. In 1908 a dismissed naval cadet George Archer-shee appealed against his dismissal in the court and eventually won the case. His fight proved his innocence and earned him a compensation. It also brought about an important procedural change in jurisprudence. A court could hear a petition against the crown after an endorsement by the attorney general with the words 'Fiat Justilia' (Let right be done') on behalf of the crown.

It is appropriate that understanding of status of a soldier forms the basis for suggestions for reformation of jurisprudence in the Indian armed forces.Military service in India is voluntary and it implies that abrogation of some fundamental rights by the soldier in higher interests of the nation/service is also voluntary. He is the defender of the Constitution and not a deprived citizen.Yet, he willingly submits himself to three sets of laws. Just as any other citizen, he is subjected to the laws of the land and enjoys no special privileges as an individual. As a member of the armed forces his service conditions and functioning are governed by the military law. Military law is devised to provide for speedy trial and disposal of breaches of discipline both in times of war and peace. It aims to act as deterrent and administer justice. It has no reformative objective. It is more severe than the laws of the land.Finally the soldier in his performance of the ultimate duty (war), he is governed by the provisions of international laws, regulations and conventions. Often heard dictum that the victor dictates the law is not true. In the civilised comity of nations, even the members of the victorious armies have been punished due to pressure of international public opinion.

There are issues in the jurisprudence of our armed forces which need to be addressed to improve the service conditions of personnel. Abrogation of fundamental rights of soldiers is one among them. There is a needless extremism while interpreting the laws, rules and regulations. Freedom of expression is denied to individuals even when it does not violate security of information. Any attempt to seek exemption is frought with cumbersome procedures. Any collective representation is viewed as mutinous behaviour (issue has been discussed in detail later in this book). Contact with foreign nationals (including those of Indian origin) is shunned. Such blanket curtailment of freedom of individuals in a routine ritualistic manner is inimical to the larger interests of democracy, military as an institution and suffocative to the individuals.

The other aspect which is cause for scepticism is the functional methodology of instruments of military jurisprudence. The existing system comprises summary trial, trial by court martial and armed forces tribunal. Functional ground reality is that these instruments are far from being fair. On many occasions the first is arbitrary, the second predetermined and the third is new and needs to be observed with guarded optimism. In a case of moral turpitude while the court martial sentenced the accused to imprisonment, the thoughtless Commander-in-Chief summarily punished seven officers associated with various stages of investigation. Such arbitrary harshness was not warranted by any norms of administration or jurisprudence. In similar vein, the convening authorities of court martial often try to predetermine the outcome and routinely misuse the provisions of military law such as exemption of witnesses. In fact on many occasions, very senior personnel need to be put in the witness box for serious lapses like loss of ship.

If ritualistic and routine abrogation of fundamental rights of defence personnel renders them a class of deprived citizen; the lopsided instruments of jurisprudence and severity of law make them instruments of tyranical administration. Further, the tendancy to exploit the instuments of jurisprudence as easy method of personnel management is deplorable.

Part- 2

Aspects relating to personnel

Part II - Aspects relating to personnel

Chapter-6

Ethical dimension of military leadership

"In war moral conditions make up three quarters of the game; the relative balance of manpower accounts for only the remaining quarter".

- Napoleon Bonaparte

So much has been written about the leadership phenomenon in the specialised literature of management and other social sciences that any more writing in similar vein would be superfluous. However, military application of this sociological phenomenon (human related function) is unique and demands its own place in any reflective writing on ethical conduct such as this book. Military experts of various periods and different societies acknowledge that 'man behind the machine' as the single most important factor in combat. Infact, artificial intelligence and automation have upgraded the man into an extremely specialised professional and placed greater demands on the leadership function. Leadership is at the very core of military professionalism because it has the potential to transform that otherwise tangible human resource into something more than what can be rationally expected from it. Wellington's comment on leadership of Napoleon too suggests the same. Military establishment seeks to maintain motivation of personnel at unusually high level so much so that the combatant not only endures extreme hardship but is also willing to make the supreme sacrifice. That is an extraordinary achievement against the human grain of self preservation and beyond the grasp of motivational theories of twentieth century. We may perhaps understand such achievements in motivation through examination of relationship between the man and body military. Nearly two centuries ago this relationship could well be regarded as contract due to mercenary attitude of the soldier and commercial attitude of the ruler or military chief. In the present day environment of aggressive nationalism it is more than mere monetary or material contract. It is to a great extent psychological and moral. The soldier is provided with a cause (often a lofty one) leading to high level of motivation and then membership of an elite and well strutctured organisation thus enhancing his pride in himself and his organisation. This motivational process involves some kind of indoctrination about the moral attributes of soldiers of civilised societies.

Organised studies to understand leadership phenomenon have progressed through 'qualities approach' ; 'situational approach' and 'functional approach'. These approaches are not radically different from each other, instead there is much overlap, refinement, reiteration and gradual progression. These studies lack exactitude due to innate nature of the subject yet they have laid bare the phenomenon. Leadership is no longer myth or mystery. It is amenable to understanding through both classical notions and scientific theories. While the former approach tends to glorify leadership, the latter renders it into an inanimate mechanism called man management. It is true that modern military leadership is to a large extent man management. The military establishment prefers the more 'functional approach' because of its suitability for selection and training. Yet, the military profession can ill-afford to neglect certain fine qualities associated with the phenomenon. These qualities represent the ethical or moral dimension of military leadership and that is the sole concern of this chapter and in consonance with the theme of the book.

An admirable military leader is essentially embodiment of certain personal qualities (latent value system) and his conduct (manifest behaviour) is an expression of these. Understanding these qualities is useful in indoctrination (training) and evaluation (appraisal) of personnel. However, the 'qualities approach' is not only less scientific but also has some drawbacks. In various spheres of human endeavour, the personality traits of successful leadership would differ depending on the nature of task, team composition and environment. For a hypothetical generalist leader the list would be unmanageable if not endless. There would be variations even in military leadership for combat roles and peacetime assignments. There is also the low probability of certain eccentricities of leaders creeping in due to over association with personality. This study aimed at isolating core values useful to body, military has adopted a modified 'qualities approach' due to its pre-eminence. The deliberations avoid too generalised treatment by restricting to crucial qualities that make the difference and rooting the exploration in reality by discussion of conduct of past personalities and events. Due to laudable objectives of the study, allegations of iconoclasm and ulterior motives are not tenable.

Courage

Although there is no rigid heirarchy based on importance, courage and sacrifice figure as the foremost among the admired qualities in a combatant. In a way these two qualities are complementary to each other and for that reason have been dealt with together. Courage covers physical, mental and moral aspects. Demonstrated courageous behaviour in the face of physical danger as in combat zone is known as bravery. Those familiar with battlefield scenario will admit that bravery in war is a common occurrence. Gallery of gallant soldiers of the Indian Army stretches from pre independence era to the present day. Many among them made the supreme sacrifice as well. In close combat situations leading from the front is regarded as appropriate behaviour. Any hesitation to adopt this model has often incited subordinates' behaviour ranging from insubordination to fragging. Mental courage involves continued pursuit of objectives even under adverse or disadvantageous conditions. However, the dividing line between courage and foolhardiness is thin. Moral courage involves decision making on ethical issues like risking the lives of subordinates and the extent of damage that can be inflicted on the enemy. The nature of sacrifice one may have to make under such situations are personal. Incidence of failure of mental or moral courage is more in peacetime assignments.

Lt Gen JFR Jacob in his autobiography narrates an incident where a Divisional Commander on inspection insisted on going too close to the line of control against the advice of Brigade Commander. When his action attracted fire by the Pakistani Rangers, he bolted in the tall grass but left behind the wounded accompanying soldier. Later he directed the Brigade Commander to destroy the machine gun position well inside Pakistani territory. If the narration is true and accurate, then it was definitely failure of physical, mental and moral courage.

Feeble resistance of Gen KS Thimayya to politicisation of the army by Krishna Menon stands out in stark contrast to the bold stand of Adm Vishnu Bhagwat against George Fernandes for similar reasons. Thimayya buckling under Nehru's pressure was lacking in moral courage and his continuation in the army thereafter may be regarded as dishonourable part in his career. However, both of them failed to mobilise support for their actions from other important institutions of democracy. To safeguard the interests of the institutions they represent is a moral obligation of the leadership.

Sacrifice

Supreme sacrifice by combatants is not uncommon. Such extreme combat behaviour is discussed in detail in a dedicated chapter titled 'Suicidal Missions'. In this chapter self sacrifice as a personal quality is discussed in general terms to obtain a rational perspective. Some instances of naval leadership responses in seemingly similar situation are listed below to evaluate propriety of conduct.

- Casabiianca stood fast on the burning deck and perished in absence of orders from his father to abandon ship.
- The Commanding Officer of *USS Pueblo* surrendered his electronic intelligence gathering ship to the enemy to avoid jeopardising the lives of crew.
- During the Indo-Pak War of 1971, Captain Mahendra Nath Mulla went down with his ship *INS Kukhri* that was damaged by enemy torpedo action.
- The Commanding Officer of *INS Andaman* abandoned his sinking ship damaged by bad weather in peacetime.

The unwavering obedience of an adolescent in the first instance was an admirable act. The youth was perhaps not capable of situational understanding and analysis. The second was a well considered decision by the Commanding Officer in the face of conflicting requirements of national security vis-a-vis loyalty to subordinates and responsibility for their lives. However, much eulogised supreme sacrifice of Captain

Mahendra Nath Mulla and abandoning of sinking ship by Commanding Officer of *INS Andaman* need to be examined with regard to circumstances, conduct of individuals and attitude of higher authorities to these incidents.

Self sacrifice in pursuit of worthwhile objectives in combat situations is an admirable act but when practised in adherence of ritualistic customs and traditions of a bygone era, it serves no purpose. Undue attachment to hardware should be discouraged. Human life and experience are more important and must be respected. Sufficient efforts must be made to safeguard the lives of subordinates in a selfless manner. Therefore, Captain Mulla's action of going down with his ship served no purpose other than avoiding a court martial for loss of ship.

Ovation of both political and military leaders who speak of 'defending to the last man and to the last drop of blood' need to be pardoned for their exhuberance of patriotic feelings or else whoever sanctioned them to authorise total annihilation of the fighting man.

Commanding Officer of *INS Andaman* was the last man to abandon his sinking ship. His conduct needs to be appreciated. The ship sank because it was not sea worthy. Therefore, all those who were responsible for her material state and those who put her to sea were guilty of misconduct.

Loyalty

Loyalty is a quality which describes a person's allegiance to individuals or institutions. Importance of this trait is that it is one of the ingredients for team building. In the military environment the aim is to develop loyalty to the institutions or organisations like country service and units.There is also the requirement of loyalty to legitimate authority. Loyalty is not unidirectional from subordinate to the superior. On the contrary it is a two way obligation. Loyalty to superior is conditional. The follower has no moral obligation to owe allegiance to a leader who indulges in wrong doing. The guideline for loyalty may be summarised as - institution first, individual next and the cause espoused is the touchstone.

Honesty

Days of cantonment soldiering are over and the soldiers have joined the mainstream of society as is apt in a democracy. In a society where corruption is rampant and all pervasive, cynicism about the moral quality of honesty is natural reaction. Hence the often heard gibe 'Honesty is lack of oppotunity'. However, soldiers need to be more proactive to uphold moral values. Involvement of very senior defence personnel in Sukhna land scam and Adarsh scam are unmistakable signs of declining moral standards in the armed forces. It is not the lucre only that drives personnel to dishonest ways. Lack of honesty of purpose is another cause. Sometime back army personnel faked encounters in order to earn personal honours and unit citations. Perpetrators of the act perhaps did not realise that fake reports could have escalated the tension with adversary.

Integrity

The *Oxford English Dictionary* renders the primary meaning of the word 'integrity' as the quality of having strong moral principles. It is obvious that the term in its broad sweep encompasses many personal qualities or moral attributes thus making it difficult to be precise as to what constitutes integrity.Yet, instead of rejecting the word as dissipated expression, it may be adopted to situations where multiple qualities coalesce to form the basis for individual conduct. Here is such an instance.

(Then) Brigadier KM Cariappa was fully aware of the non-violent nationalist movement for independence and also the aspirations of the nascent nation to adopt democratic norms of governance. Yet, he volunteered a suggestion to Lord Ismay (a close advisor to Viceroy Mountbatten) that the Indian Army with either Nehru or Jinnah as the Commander-in-Chief should take over power from the British. The act could be termed as lacking in integrity, the only hesitation being that the suggestion came from one of the most revered military leaders of India. A military leader needs to be uncompromising in his moral values or else subordinates are unlikely to hold such persons in high esteem.

Unfortunately there is no dedicated training curriculum in our armed forces for developing the moral attributes of leadership phenomenon.Officers responsible for training show no inclination or interest in this aspect. On induction into the Armed Forces, seniors and peer groups forcibly indoctrinate juniors to develop ' a code of convenience ' under the guise of smartening up process. The void is filled, not with virtue but by the vicious.

Chapter-7

Concept of martial classes and gender related issues

"Historically speaking, the Punjab is a British myth; and no more the special home of a fighting race than anywhere else in India. Over the centuries historical greatness of India was never identified with a strong Punjab"

Pannikar
Eminent historian

Indian armed forces existed long before independence due to colonial past but their status and functional ethos as forces serving colonial masters vis-a-vis serving the national flag of a secular democracy varied significantly. Yet, the armed forces prefer to retain some of their traditional practices (customs and traditions are very important to military). In this writing two discriminatory practices of personal management where traditions, socio-cultural norms and military pragmatism are in conflict with constitutional propriety are discussed. One is the concept of martial classes through which Indian army organises majority of infantry troops on socio-religious basis. The other is gender related discrimination in employment of women in all three services. The word discrimination in this context refers to differential treatment and has no suggestion or connotation of malevolent attitude either by establishment or individuals. Infact, in the second instance there is a positive attitude of considerate and deferential treatment of women. The objective of these deliberations is to seek some kind of rationalisation and facilitate transformation rather than highlighting the conflict situation.

Recognition of military as an essential instrument of statecraft led to early evolution of function based warrior class. In the ancient Indian history, the class was known as *Kshatriya* (a caste). This caste was widely spread across the Indian sub continent and had no specific geographical or ethnic origin. Selection to the profession was based on soldierly attributes of the individual. The practice of classifying social groups into martial or non martial classes is of British origin based on twin considerations of unwavering loyalty and combat worthy human resources. However, in the aftermath of Sepoy Mutiny (First War of Independence 1857) the British became acutely concerned about the loyalty of troops. They created vested interest groups through systematic discriminatory process. The troops were very well looked after and were kept insulated from mainstream of the society in general and the Indian nationalist movement in particular. The other measure was to restrict recruitment to some socio-religious groups and classify them as martial classes. Despite such discriminatory process, the British did not experience any difficulty in recruiting the required number due to availability of vast manpower resources on the Indian sub continent. Infact, as part of their war effort, British managed to raise a two million strong army without recourse to conscription.

System of class composition as a criterion for recruitment to any particular branch did not exist for other two services as combat situations are totally different. If in the Navy, there was concentration of sailors from Konkan coast (Ratnagiri area) in the gunnery branch or sailors from Malabar coast (Kerala) in the communication branch. It was based on purely, skills and attributes.

In the Air Force combat role of the pilots is restricted to officers and those other than pilots form the logistic infrastructure away from the combat zone. Even in the army the system is prevalent only in infantry regiments. Although the system is a vestige of colonial past, it is not without merits.

When selection to a particular regiment is restricted to a small geographical area or close knit socio-religious groups, then there is a high degree of commonality amongst individuals with regard to religion or caste, culture, language and even dietary preference. The successive generations of the community or families serve in the same unit or regiment. The request of individual to serve in the same unit as his forefathers is respected by the institution and is known as parental claim in the military parlance. The above stated considerations have far greater appeal and are more potent motivators than the ideals enshrined in a secular democratic constitution. Battle cries of some of the regiments prove the point.

Battle cries of some Infantry Regiments (In Roman Hindi / Vernacular)

Maratha Light Infantry :

Bolo Chhatrapathi Shivaji Maharaj Ki Jai

Sikh Regiment :

Bolo so nihal sat sri akal

Waheh guruji ka khalsa, Waheh guruji ki fateh

Jat Regiment :

Jai bhagawan, Jat balawan

Gurkha Regiment :

Jai mahakali, Ayo Gorkhali

Administratively too the system is a great convenience as it is easier to manage the logistics associated with homogenous groups.

However, there are two valid reservations about the above discussed system - one constitutional and the other political. The idea of organising regiments along socio-religious or regional considerations is not congruent with the concept of national army of a secular democracy. A national army should ideally be true representative institution not by quota allocation or reservation but by open recruitment irrespective of religion or region. Denial of opportunity to a citizen to serve in an unit or organisation of his own choice merely on these grounds is repugnant. If the constitutional objection is in the realms of idealism, the political objection is rooted in the ground reality of administrative unsuitability.

In 1950 India was reorganised into union of states based on linguistic basis. Subsequent sub divisions were also made for administrative or ethnic considerations. The division of the country into states in some instances also approximates the socio-religious divide. The often heard rhetoric of unity amidst diversity is actually wishful thinking of Indian statesmen. The ground reality is that the sub continent is a classroom model of various forms of irregular warfare with equally diverse objectives of seeking socio-economic justice, autonomy, secession and independence. Indian army has been almost continuously been engaged in internal security duties to combat these incidences of irregular warfare. Employing troops to fight their own kind is not only a dangerous proposition but may also incite mutinous behaviour. Under such conditions desirability of employing mixed troops can not be contested.

Attempts have been made to raise mixed troops but with limited success. The first such attempt was made by (then) General Cariappa in raising the Guards Regiment. The process was hampered by some senior officers who were none too enthusiastic about the change. A repeat attempt was made while commissioning mechanised infantry units. There is an inherent resistance to change in all institutions but armed forces are aggressive to preserve their traditional values. In similar vein as class based organisation of regiments, the army of secular India employs religious preachers of major religions as enlisted men. The rationale for this practice is not clearly stated. Reasons offered vary from meeting spiritual and religious needs of men to maintain the morale and motivation of troops. It will be an achievement for Indian Army when its mixed troops are guided and motivated by home grown 'Military Philosophy' derived from the constitution of the country and humanism.

The second discriminatory process which has incurred wrath of female members of armed forces and some outsiders too is the gender related bias in employment and service conditions of women in the armed forces. While some have sought legal remedy to this discrimination, there are debates in the media about the same.The factual situation is that constitutional propriety is in conflict with socio-cultural norms and military pragmatism. In the bygone era, choice of profession and nature of employment for women were guided by gender attributes like physical capabilities, feminine skills and psychological factors. Similarly the task of bearing arms for the country fell to the lot of male members in the society. Education and legislation have empowered the present day Indian women to seek equality with men in all walks of life. Even the last bastion of masculinity (armed forces) has been invaded, although the number of women being admitted is restricted in terms of number, branch or specialisation and the roles asigned to them. These three issues are discussed below to highlight the rationale of these restrictions.

As of now women are admitted to only the officer cadre in all three services. Further, they perform what could logically be called support roles like administration including legal services, logistics, training and medical duties. Even when permitted on other duties like flying, it is restricted to transport and helicopters. They are not exposed to combat roles and, therefore, occupy 'peaceful billets'. There is the service requirement to rotate personnel between operational and peacetime billets for reasons of training, maintenance, medical and welfare requirements. That is the basis for restricting the number of women to a certain percentage of overall strength.

Feminists who translate gender equality as gender blind uniformity go wrong on many counts. Physiological and psychological differences between male and female which make women unsuitable for combat roles is a reality and not a bias. Brutal conditions of combat zone are at times unimaginable. No civilised society would like to induct its women soldiers into combat zone where even devils dread to tread. At war crimes tribunal charges like sexual harassment, abuse and sexual enslavement are not uncommon. Some depraved soldiers may even consider these offences as forms of warfare. It is not the enemy alone, even their own male colleagues may commit crimes like sexual harrasment and rape.

It is an acknowledged fact that even in the elite armed forces, a large percentage of gender or sex related offences go unreported due to reasons varying from non-conformity of regulations by females to social stigma attached to the occurrence. Therefore, women being denied combat roles are not being discriminated but are being protected.

Advocacy of uniformity and opening combat roles for women soldiers is at times advanced through wrong examples. The militaries of three countries which have removed all restrictions on employment of women soldiers namely Australia, NewZealand and Canada; by and large, see no combat action. Israel, a nation which percieves existential threat to its very existence is another nation which adopts similar approach.

The attitude of the military establishment in this country to the two issues have been deliberated upon adequately. However, changes in the prevalent system may be warranted by societal changes. The process of change (particularly in this area) is slow and has to march a step behind societal changes. Only persons with understanding of the spirit of Indian Constitution; importance of customs and traditions to armed forces and military pragmatism can chart the roadmap for transformation and facilitate the process.

Chapter-8

Political education and unionisation of soldiers

"Good ideas are not adopted automatically. They must be driven into practice with courageous patience."

- Hyman Rickover

Armed forces who strive to remain at the fore front of combat technology through continuous modernisation, ironically freeze into conservatism at any suggestion of changes in service conditions of its personnel. In their earnest desire for stability, they prefer status quo and in stock response resist change. Any community which aspires to grow should be receptive to change. Momentum of change provides stability to a community in motion. The Indian armed forces due to this attitudinal bondage refuse to recognise political education and unionisation of soldiers as important instruments (interventions) of human resource development.

Transformation of a soldier from hired mercenary (and often a social outcast too) to a citizen soldier has been a saga of approximately two centuries in terms of time span, otherwise it has altered the very basis of his service to the state.In our times soldier has become much venerated icon of aggressive nationalism. To a soldier of twentyfirst century serving the national flag of democracy, political education is an important enabling process to guide him on the propriety of his conduct.Yet, many in the Indian armed forces apprehensively regard political education of soldiers a needless provocation which can lead to politicisation of armed forces.Such apprehensions result from mistaken perception which equates political education with political indoctrination. There is a subtle difference between the two. Political indoctrination prevalent in communist or such other oppressive regimes compels individuals to accept particular political idealogy and to work for the same. Political education strives to promote understanding of the letter and spirit of the constitutional provisions, functional modalities, the basis of his service to the state and the importance of his apolitical conduct.

All countries maintain armed forces which are nationalistic in character and membership is open to all citizens subject to suitability and selection. Countries which enrol non-nationals, offer them citizenship.

Usually the service is voluntary but at times some countries resort to conscription due to demographic reasons. Soldiers on admission are administered an oath of allegiance to the Constitution of the land and obedience to the head of state. The essence of the oath is loyalty and obedience to authority. The oath administered to the Indian soldiers is reproduced below.

Oath of Allegiance

I do swear in the name of God and solemnly affirm that I will bear true faith and allegiance to the Constitution of India as by law established and that I will, as in duty bound, honestly and faithfully serve in the Navy / Army / Air Force of the Union of India and go wherever ordered by sea, land or air and that I will observe and obey all commands of the President of India and commands of any officer set over me even to the peril of my life.

Prime loyalty of the Indian soldier is to the Constitution of India. All other loyalties whether to any authority, individual or religion rank lower. However this situational clarity fades into a grey shade when the soldier is faced with multiple value systems in force or in an emotionally surcharged situation. Majority of infantry troops in the Indian army are organised on martial class concept which in some cases happen to be religion/caste based too. Sikh troops on induction into service are administered both civil (constitution) and religious (Guru Granth Sahib) oaths. There were sporadic instances of mutinuous behaviour by sikh soldiers in the aftermath of Operation Blue Star. These episodes were dismissed as emotional exhuberance without analysing the genesis of such behaviour.

Unexplained contradictions also cause doubts. A significant number of non-Indian nationals (Nepali Gorkhas) serve in the Indian armed forces. Historically, the entire sub continent was part of British empire and Gorkhas were recruited in large numbers as the British regarded them as loyal and trustworthy fighting men. In the post independence era the system continued in accordance with tripartite agreement. What is their status and the rationale for such stance? However, with abolition of Nepalese monarchy, the prospect of continued recruitment of Gurkhas into the Indian army is in doubt. Communist Party of Nepal (Maoist) regards Nepalese serving as mercenaries degrading and has proposed to ban the same.

The issue of obedience to authority is closely linked to loyalty. It is suitable to begin deliberations on the issue with reiteration of constitutional basis of inter institutional relations and exercise of power. President of the Indian Union is also the supreme commander of Indian armed forces. He is the notional head to stress on the autonomous status and spirit of military as an institution of democracy rather than any realtime exercise of power. Defence minister, who is a representative of political executive is the Chief Executive of the armed forces and the functional head. Some recent events from the Indian experiment with parliamentary democracy are narrated to demonstrate that even a lengthy constitution does not suffice as a set of ground rules for those who tread the politico-military domain.

In the aftermath of Allahabad High Court indicting Indira Gandhi guilty of corrupt election practices there was a clamour for her resignation. It was essentially a political wrangle between her and Janata Morcha Alliance led by Jayaprakash Narayan (JP). JP appealed to police and the armed forces not to obey illegal and immoral orders of the government. Indira Gandhi proclaimed national emergency through obliging President Fakhruddin Ali Ahmed. She also made subtle suggestions to the army to act as enforcers of emergency. In this volatile situation, apolitical stance of the army and its Chief General T.N. Raina averted the derailing of Indian democracy. Years later, a researcher (Apurba Kundu) who examined the episode found that among the top brass of the army there were sympathisers, empathisers and opponents of Indira Gandhi. That is an indication of multiple possibilities in the politico-military domain.

In another instance it was rumoured that the relationship between the then President Giani Zail Singh and Prime Minister Rajiv Gandhi had soured to such an extent that Zail Singh was toying with the idea of dismissing Rajiv Gandhi with the help of army. Fact that nothing came of it was a big relief to the Indian democracy.

Incidents such as narrated above are traumatic experiences for democracy and testing time for the rectitude of military leadership.Propriety of ethical conduct for soldiers in such circumstances is a very fine line and they have to tread it with utmost balance to acquit themselves honourably. It will serve them well to know that arbitration in inter institutional conflicts is not their legitimate role. They may intervene only when national security or integrity are endangered.

> *"What is conservatism? Is it not the adherence to the old and tried against the new and untried?".*
>
> **- Abraham Lincoln**

Many third world countries may not have evolved politically despite democratic norms of governance being in vogue. Disorder and indiscipline are common occurrences. In such political communities, the military establishment is regarded as the last bastion of orderliness and efforts are made to insulate it from outside influence.

Military on their part are steeped into conservatism and regard unionisation of soldiers as sacrilege of military ethos and inimical to the interests of discipline. In yet another stance of stock response collective representation (particularly dissent) is considered mutinous behaviour. The abysmal level to which the union activities have degenerated has caused loss of faith in the process and provided crude justification to spurn the otherwise useful process. Since the term 'unionisation' has fallen into disrepute, its resurrection is best handled by initiating a marketing process called 'objection handling'.

A major apprehension among both civil society and the military establishment about unionisation of soldiers is that it may lead to politicisation and undermine the apolitical character of our armed forces. It need not be so. If abrogation of fundamental rights of soldiers does not lead to enslavement, why should unionisation lead to politicisation? The functional methodology of 'soldiers' union' needs to be regulated.

Banning political affiliation, forbidding outsider influence or participation and permitting single union will definitely sanitise operational environment of the union. It is a fallacy to equate collective representation with militant mutinous behaviour. Contrarily, collective representation provides an avenue for two way interaction for resolution of common (group) issues. Perhaps mutiny on board ships of Western Fleet in 1974 (due to wrong scheduling of sailing programme) and mutiny in the Indian Air Force in 1998 (due to faulty wage structure) could have been averted had collective representation been in vogue. Therefore, collective representation does not lead to indiscipline, instead it provides a safety vent and startles unresponsive management into positive action.

Participative management (union may be regarded as a special form of participative management) is not new to the armed forces, but is adopted in a restricted manner for informal systems functioning within the formal framework of armed forces like operation of messes, institutes (clubs) and welfare schemes. Even in these instances performance is sub optimal due to obsession of military authorities to exercise stranglehold over organisational functioning. To widen the scope and increase the efficacy of participative management, it should be introduced in deciding the service conditions. In fact there is no justifiable rationale for denying participation to personnel in this vital area. It is worth noting that some western armed forces permit their personnel to collectively express their opinion even in operational matters. The approach is more appropriate as armed forces are increasingly being deployed in 'war of values' as distinct from 'war of interests' or 'territorial conflicts'.

The purpose of these deliberations is to advocate exploitation of the process of unionisation as an innovative and useful intervention of human resource management and for valid reasons too. The process will find favour with members of the organisation due to its democratic method and also result in synergy between political ethos and military functioning.

Part-3

Combat philosophy

Part III - Combat Philosophy

Chapter 9: Nature of War

Chapter 10: Perspectives in combat philosophy

Chapter 11: Suicidal Missions

Chapter-9

Nature of War

"There never was a good war or bad peace"

- Benjamin Franklin

"If you hear the details of victory,

it is hard to distinguish it from defeat"

- Jean-Paul Sartre

War is undoubtedly a complex activity which is influenced by and also influences many spheres of human endeavour. In the past, wars have mobilised societies, spurred industrial growth and development of technology, eroded national economies and even affected demography of societies. The geo-political outcomes of war are equally wide ranging—geographical boundaries of nations are altered, new nations are born, different political ideologies are ushered in and new political alignments and alliances come into being. War has also served as a laboratory and classroom for many areas of learning, particularly the management discipline which has liberally borrowed from its lexicon. Wartime destruction and damage have formed the foundation of nation building activities. Frenzied nationalism and emotions have inspired literary creativity. At times even national psyche is affected.

In the aftermath of 9/11 terrorist attack on the US, the anguished American President George W Bush called it an act of dastardly cowardice. The response clearly failed to recognise the characteristics and significance of the strike. It was an irregular form of warfare (terrorism) and had deliberately struck at the very roots of American pride. The attackers had carefully chosen their targets - Pentagon (military prowess), World Trade Centre (economic strength) and the failed attempt on White House (egalitarian political ideology). The attack also exposed American vulnerability to irregular forms of warfare. Then French President Jacques Chirac gave better account of terrorism while expressing his anguish over the same incident. However, soldiers cannot indulge in such emotional exhuberance. SOLDIERS MUST KNOW HOW TO WAGE OR COMBAT WAR IN ANY OF ITS MUTANT MANIFESTATIONS. That is a professional demand and necessity.

While soldierly response to warlike or conflict situation is made possible through understanding of a complex and multi-dimensional phenomenon called war, optimism prompts us to believe that conflicts can be de-escalated and evils of war mitigated. Study of warfare may fascinate scholars of Military History but is essential to soldiers in leadership roles who need to understand their legitimate role and ethical aspects of their conduct. Such study would include causal inquiry of wars, significance of conflict spectrum and prevalent value system in the domain of their operation. This writing is not an exhaustive study of warfare, far from that, it is a limited and modest description of the domain context to facilitate deliberations on the thematic concern of this book, namely ethical code of conduct for soldiering.

What is war?

"War is continuation of politics by other means"

- Clauswitz

The above Clauswitzian dictum may be rephrased to explain the phenomenon (War) as state of hostilities between two or more political communities. Participation by more than two political communities and thus escalating the war from bilateral to multi-lateral needs no examples or elaboration as history of warfare is replete with such instances. In any case the great war is too fresh in our memory. Our preference for the expression 'political communities' instead of 'nation states' does need justification. With proliferation of irregular forms of warfare and increased frequency of their incidence, it is most likely that the adversary in conflict may not be a state entity. Ideological groups who may have wide geographical spheres of influence and possess capabilities to wage irregular wars may not be state entities with clearly demarcated, political and geographical boundaries. An apt example would be the war being waged by Islamic fundamental groups on America, Western nations and their interests and the American response in the form of 'War on Terror'. Then there is also the growing inclination to replace the word 'War' by 'Conflict situation' under some circumstances. Waging and combating some forms of irregular warfare may involve actions which are not warlike. Further, politico-diplomatic compulsions in the comity of nations may not permit or be suitable for formal declaration of war.

War has been an integral part of human civilisation since antiquity. Attempt to date the event will be futile and in any case serve no purpose in this study. Initially, war involving use of armed force started as essential instrument or function to protect societies. Over the ages it acquired complexity and its operating modes evolved to include aggression,intervention and enforcement. Survey of twentieth century wars reveals that adversaries in conflict have been superpowers, regional powers, small nation states and in some cases non-state entities. Economically too, the participants have been developed, developing and underdeveloped nations. Both nuclear and non-nuclear powers have also had their share of wars. The saving grace has been that super powers and nuclear powers have not had any direct confrontations. This widespread and timeless phenomenon compels anyone associated or interested in military matters to probe it further to understand the relationship between causes, types of warfare adopted and status of the adversaries involved in the conflict.

Why do wars occur?

"The purpose of all wars is peace"

- Saint Augustine

> *"Wars end not due to peace processes, but due to one side giving up"*
>
> **- Daniel Pipes**

At the functional level war is essentially an instrument of last resort for conflict resolution between nations. The outcome of the war is unlikely to be satisfactory for both or all parties and also may not bring lasting peace or permanent settlement of the dispute. The outcome of the resolution would depend on multiple factors like war making capability of the adversaries, role of international bodies or mediators, and the cause of conflict itself. There have been several causes of war in the past but no chronological order is evident.

The most fundamental cause of war between nations has been contesting claims of territory. Although the territorial boundaries of nation states in Europe acquired relative finality in the post world war era, some disputes do exist among third world countries which emerged from the decolonisation process. Some of these disputes have led to regional wars and yet remain unresolved. In some cases disputes have not remained purely bilateral due to interference by third party or extra regional powers.

Disintegration of the erstwhile Soviet Union in the latter part of twentieth century resulted in new nation states at war with each other. An extension of territorial disputes is the competition or rivalry of nations to access economic resources, both continental and maritime. During the age of discovery and subsequently, this competition between European powers led to colonisation of third world countries rich in natural resources. Even piracy gained respectability through state patronage. This was also the period of pure maritime wars.

Wars and conflicts between communities or societies due to religious and ethnic sensibilities ranging from unacceptability, intolerance to hatred have been part of history of mankind. The author does not know with certainty the role of religion in ancient civilisations, but from medieval times religion has been a core value; potent motivator of both citizens and soldiers; of profound influence on politics and of course, one of the major causes of war. The animus between Christianity and Islam, for instance, is an undeniable fact of history as demonstrated by the following advice of Pope Pius II to Mohammed II, the conqueror of Constantinople in 1460 AD. "You are not so ignorant of our affairs that you do not know the power of Christian people - of Spain so steadfast, Gaul so warlike, Germany so populous, Britian so strong, Poland so daring, Hungary so active and Italy so rich, high spirited and experienced in the art of war". The mutual distrust and dislike between Islam and Christianity is not merely a historical fact but continues to date.In the modern secular Indian state too there have been religion and ethnicity based and inspired militancies aimed at secession. However, the civilised world today accepts secularism as one of the tenable core values for interaction between nation states either in earnest belief or for reasons of political correctness. George Bush described the American response and the resolve to combat terrorism as 'crusade' initially and subsequently used toned down expressions like 'war for civilisation'; 'a task that never ends'; 'war against global terror' and 'titanic war on terror'. Whether it was toned down rhetoric or political correctness is debatable.

The industrial revolution ushered in material prosperity but was also cause of an important sociological change. It divided the society into classes thus sowing the seeds of communism. The idealogical divide between democracy and communism was further accentuated in the post world war era, precipitating cold war and freezing the world into rigid political blocks. Although, the cold war was a non-event, it did cause hindrance to the functioning of the world body in establishing lasting peace and harmonious comity of nations.

The above in general are the causes of war or conflict between political communities. When simmering hostilities between two nations are already on the brink, then even single event or incident such as hijacking, hostage taking or any other heinous crime may spark conflicts. Usually the response or retaliation is swift surgical like operation for immediate resolution of the conflict. Yet such operations have the potential to escalate the conflict to prolonged and full fledged war. Large scale atrocities committed by the Pakistan Army on Bangladeshis and large influx of refugees into India triggered Indo-Pak War of 1971.

Spectrum of conflict

"Every incident of irregular warfare is a new form in itself due to wide variance in circumstances, objectives, motives and methods"

- Author

Some military writers arrange forms of warfare into a 'ladder of conflict' based on incremental escalation of violence or geographical extent. For holistic approach to classifying types of warfare it is suitable to arrange all considerations in a rainbow type spectrum of conflict.

The open ended spectrum may be divided into two segments namely regular and irregular warfare. The adversaries in regular war would be clearly identifiable political communities (nation states) or alliances of such entities. Depending on whether the conflict is bilateral or multilateral and the geographical extent of the combat zone wars may be classified as interstate, regional or global. Munition used would distinguish between nuclear and conventional wars. The segment of regular wars would also include cold war (non-event) and civil war (intrastate conflict). High level of nuclear proliferation precipitated deterrence and cold war. At this juncture 'cold war' may seem an archiac lexicon from the bygone era of US-Soviet confrontation, but the possibility of its re-emergence in future cannot be ruled out. Discontent and exploitation in autocratic and oppressive regimes may result in revolts or civil wars. Although some of the civil wars may adopt irregular forms of war, civil war is classified as regular war due to dominant consideration of geographically well demarcated area.

Holistic Rainbow Spectrum of Conflict

BASIS OF CLASSIFICATION					
Geographical Extent	Global	Regional	Interstate	Intra-state	Anywhere without Geographical Limitation..............
Form of Warfare	REGULAR				IRREGULAR
	Cold	Nuclear	Conventional	Civil (Revolt)	Guerilla Terroism Insurgency Subversion and other low Intensity Operations.....................
Possible Causes	Idealogical	Territorial	Economic	Discontent exploitation	Perceived injustice and exploitation Pathological
Organisation	Clear organisational structure both for warmaking and politico-diplomatic management				Organisational and command structure not easily discernible/identifiable..................

It is noteworthy that irregular warfare segment is open ended. Every incident of irregular warfare is a new form in itself due to wide variance in circumstances, objectives, motives and methods so much so that they defy attempts to define. An exponent of irregular warfare will find it difficult to go beyond some broad generalisations. These generalisations are the basis of understanding irregular warfare.

Soldiers (practitioners) of various forms of irregular warfare don no uniform or insignia of any clearly identified political community or military formation. In fact, anonymity of individuals and their organisational affiliation is their intrinsic strength. They claim or disown responsibility for incidents to suit their objectives. Their combat zone or target area is unspecified and usually indulge in low intensity operations. Quite often the choice of targets has symbolic significance. Practitioners are committed to the cause, their motivational levels are high and frequently adopt extreme combat behaviour like suicidal missions. Their organisational structure for administration and operations is not easily discernible or identifiable rendering them invulnerable to attack.

It is important to note that in matter such as this, classification can not be rigid or absolute. For instance, due to proliferation of nuclear weapons, the possibility of tactical nuclear weapons falling in the hands of extremist or fundamentalist groups can not be ruled out. Their use in irregular warfare is a distinct possibility.

War as a recurrent phenomenon

"The most persistent sound which reverberates through humanity's history is the beating of war drums"

- Arthur Koestler

Mankind in its earnest desire for peace may consign hundred years war and World Wars to the realms of history but Pakistan made a provocative statement about waging a thousand years war against India. Churchillian prophesy that Second World War was a war to end all wars fell by the wayside as twentieth century witnessed a large number of wars. Even the first decade of the present century has not been free of wars. Destructive potential of nuclear weapons may have achieved nuclear deterrence but conventional wars continue to occur. United Nations Organisation has failed to prevent wars like its predecessor League of Nations. If there be any indication about the future, then it is the reassertion of inevitability of wars due to frailty of individuals and nations. War, over the ages, has emerged as an important institution of civilisation though its evil face makes it appear as a paradox. It nevertheless is a necessary evil and is used as the last resort (in most cases) instrument of coercive diplomacy.

Warfare has evolved over the ages. Yet the past re-asserts itself in new ways and in many ways. We optimistically believed that religious wars belonged to the past but, it is back with all its monstrosity in the garb of fundamentalism. If there is any change, the intensity of hatred has increased. Similarly, we believed that mercenary service in the military was a medieval practice and that nationalism would be the basis for military service in future. Surprisingly the mercenary service is back in the form of security firms. Western nations who enjoy material prosperity and find it difficult and costly to recruit and embody their own citizens in regular military service or the sight of body bags has tremendous adverse influence on politics at home, find it easier to outsource some of the military related tasks to 'soldiers of fortune' (private operators) from third world countries.

In the aftermath of Second World War the mankind was convinced that the Nazi's had reached the Nadir of brutality and hoped that Nuremberg trials would down the curtains on such human degradation for ever. Unfortunately, the atrocities committed by the elite soldiers of the foremost democracy on the hapless Iraqi prisoners demonstrate that human degradation and depravity are bottomless pit.

Wars are inevitable, the effects undesirable and the outcomes are the seeds of future wars. The adversaries in the conflict may hail from widely differing ethnic, religious and cultural denominations with different value systems. Mankind needs to make earnest endeavours to establish the bottomline for soldierly conduct in combat if we wish to be regarded as civilisation by the future generations.

Chapter-10

Perspectives in combat philosophy

"Because of European military traditions which have found acceptance over the last two or three centuries, war has often come to be regarded as international gladiatorial contest to be fought according to international rules and laws".

-PVR Rao

in *Defence Without Drift*

The members of the 'body military' are guided by the constitution and laws of the land in their interactions with other important institutions of democracy, whereas their personal conduct is governed by the special laws enacted by the government. However, while operating in combat zone (war), they are governed by the additional jurisprudence of international laws and conventions. Their actions are closely monitored by national and international humanitarian watchdog agencies and the media. Therefore, often heard colloquials like 'All is fair in Love and War' or 'Victor dictates the law' are merely euphemistic justification of unscruplous and unsoldierly behaviour, perhaps prompted by the tardy implementation of international laws and conventions. Frequently, non-state entities in combat show no inclination to observe these rules. Yet, legalities of the situation is not the only burdensome constraint of the soldiers. Heightened emotions and short reaction times make sane and rational behaviour difficult to maintain. If war is an integral institution of human civilisation, then the dilemma of the paradox has to be resolved by the soldiers. Awareness and understanding of ethical norms is useful in guiding the spontaneous responses of the combatants.

Although, this book is concerned with the rectitude of soldiers both in war and peace, issues related to combat are treated as separate domain and titled 'Combat Philosophy' to facilitate better understanding and coherent rendering. The division can not be rigid due to obvious reasons. This chapter endeavours to delineate the domain extent of combat philosophy, identify various issues involved and speculate on appropriate conduct in such situations. It is not possible to enumerate all the contingencies nor can the suggested code of conduct be enunciated in terms of rigid do's and dont's. However, deliberations on value basis should illuminate the area, which will enable soldiers to make informed decisions. Finally, a write-up on the admirable qualities in combat should help soldiers to shed false notions and act deliberately.

Domain extent of combat philosophy

"Morality may consist solely in the courage of making a choice"

- Leon Blum

The expression 'Combat Philosophy' is suggestive of pertaining to conduct of soldiers in restricted tactical domain and essentially it is so. However, clear and precise delineation of domain may not be possible due to overlapping responsibilties between bodies military and polity. Certain events and issues may pertain to the tactical domain, but there is also the state's (polity) obligation to conform to international laws and conventions for conduct of hostilities. Propensity of higher (nuclear) weapons to cause widespread destruction blurs the boundary line between strategic and tactical domains and stretches responsibility to multiple levels. These are only two instances which demonstrate that political and military power are not clearly divisible at all times. The power, therefore, may need to be wielded jointly with understanding and respect for each other. Yet, generalised delineation of domains based on responsibilities and functional requirements of both institutions is possible.

Acceptance of the postulate 'war is politics by other means' behoves a dominant decision making role for the polity in strategic or politico-military domain. In this domain issues relating to Higher Direction of War like justification for waging war, extent and type of warfare to be adopted and use of higher (nuclear) weapons are deliberated upon and decisions taken. Hence the role of military is to render professional advice. The nature of advice may vary from suggestive to assertive posturing depending as much on the efficacy of national security management mechanism as personality traits of individuals in the domain. Generally professional military advice is accepted with grace by an understanding polity (government) but there have also been instances of informed military playing suppliant role while ignorant polity being adamantly assertive.

Humiliating defeat of the Indian Army at the hands of Chinese in 1962 was in great measure attributable to the thoughtless forward policy with no logistic back-up. The government bulldozed the feeble resistance of the Army, in gross violation of functional norms promoted officers who supported the policy and precipitated the first civil-military relations crisis in India. Later, when the forward border posts were run over by the Chinese, neither Prime Minister Nehru nor the Defence Minister Krishna Menon had the grace to accept moral responsibility for the Himalayan blunder. The above governmental conduct was in total contrast to that in Bangladesh operations in 1971. The operations were delayed by as much as nine months on the recommendation of Field Marshall Manekshaw. The conduct of two important military personalities in the above episodes - meek General Thapar, who accepted bureaucrat's directive to evict the Chinese (No senior cabinet member was available at New Delhi) and Field Marshall Manekshaw who asserted his professional advice also stand out in contrast. It is always desirable that senior soldiers operating in the politico-military domain tender their professional advice without fear or favour; sought or unsolicited and in unambiguous terms. It is in the country's highest interest.

While operating in the tactical domain (combat zone) where a decision may make a difference between life or death; victory or defeat; morale or dishonour, then it is the field commander who should prevail.

Observance of laws of war (international regulations and conventions), ethical code of conduct or any other established norms is undoubtedly the legitimate professional and moral responsibility of the field commanders at varying levels. Ostensibly, polity has no role in this domain. However, when the armed forces are deployed to combat incidents of irregular warfare like insurgency and terrorism on their own territory, then the government may attempt to intervene in pursuit of its political objectives. On such occasions any governmental directive not in agreement with professional demands should be resisted and rejected.

Operation Blue Star conducted by the Indian Army is examined as an illustrative example in the light of above recommended rectitude. It was not an operation in aid of civil administration where the guiding principle in use of force is restraint. The adversary in the conflict was fully armed and fortified. They had declared war against the Indian state in very explicit manner. It was an armed insurgency aimed at seccession. Irrespective of the location, the soldiers were fighting an insurgency (a form of irregular warfare) and under those circumstances enjoyed legitimate right to self defence and freedom of action. Yet, the Indian government directed the

Indian Army to exercise restraint to gain political advantage over the Akali leadership but placing the army in a disadvantageous position. Consequently the Army suffered heavy casualties. Later, a senior officer involved in the operations commented - "We entered the Golden Temple with humility in our hearts and prayers on our lips". In retrospect all that may be said is that it was unsoldierly behaviour. Nothing forbids a soldier from regarding this conduct as lack of concern if not of betrayal by his superiors.

Unfortunately, the Indian demographic diversity of ethnicity, religion and language; uneven economic development between regions and scant opportunities has become *casus belli* for irregular warfare.

Unfriendly neighbours are only too happy to fan the flames of dissension. The situation is so bad that the Indian Army is continuously engaged in combating insurgency, terrorism, secession and other forms of irregular warfare. Strenuous employment for prolonged periods and high casualty rates are demoralising enough, but to deny freedom of action by withdrawing legal protection is unfair to the combatants. The soldiers are not on policing duties, they are fighting a war. Any attempt to withdraw or dilute Armed Forces Special Powers Act needs to be thwarted because there are no trade offs between tactical advantage and political considerations. To the military leadership advantage to the troops and their safety should be the highest concern and not the political advantage to the government. At this point of deliberations, return to seek clarity regarding the intended meaning of the term 'politics' in the Clauswitzian dictum is necessary because of the evolutionary changes in the nature of war and adversaries involved in the conflict. The term implies interaction with recognised political communities (nation states) and not the non-state entities involved in irregular warfare.

Issues in combat philosophy

"The facts of war are inescapable - death and random cruelty, suspension of civilised values and a disordered aftermath......War remains the decisive human failure"

- JK Galbraith
Erstwhile US Ambassador to India

"In a modern war you will die like a dog for no good reason"

- Ernest Hemmingway
Writer and War correspondent

Battlefield conditions do brutalise soldiers. Driven as much by hatred for the enemy as by fear and self preservation motives, even the elite armed forces of civilised societies indulge in revulsive behaviour that can shock the conscience of sane persons. Psychological dimension of conduct of combatants in hostile or war situations is perhaps a vast area of study by itself because human perversity is no less diverse than creativity, but it is clearly beyond the scope of this monograph. Here the deliberations are restricted to enumerating the possible contingencies and a combatant's conduct under such circumstances. To a great extent, the dominant issues in combat philosophy have their genesis in the dogs of war. Death, Destruction and disorder are the lasting scars borne by the war ravaged societies. These issues are discussed below in that order.

Death in warzone is common occurrence involving both soldiers and civilians. Death of civilians may be as collateral damage or due to deliberate killing by revengeful soldiers. While the humanitarian law and considerations recommend that collateral damage be minimised through adoption of safer tactics (methods) and choice of weaponry; deliberate killing of unarmed civilians is absolutely forbidden. The latter guideline is of particular relevance while combating low intensity operations or other forms of irregular warfare. Revengeful, deliberate and mass killings, apart from being unethical, also alienate civil population and hence counter productive. Such killings do not result in submission, much less elicit cooperation. On the contrary it may trigger violent retribution and enhance the task at hand manifold. Death of combatants can result from enemy action or due to participation in suicidal missions. While the former is inevitable, the latter practice deserves separate treatment and therefore has been dealt in greater detail in the next chapter. There are many occasions when unscruplous soldiers may prefer to kill the surrendered prisoners of war due to non-feasibility of maintaining them in accordance with international regulations. The practice is ethically and legally indefensible.

There are other abhorrent practices connected with death like mutilation and body harvesting although their occurrence is less frequent. Unfortunate it may be but such barbaric conduct does have some mythological or historical precedents. In the Indian Epic of Mahabharat, Draupadi the polyandrous spouse of Pandavas, demands of Bhima (one of her husbands) that her dishevelled hair be annointed with blood of

Dusshasan for having humiliated her. There is a similar instance in the early history of Islam where a muslim woman belonging to one of the warring factions demands a cup of blood of the adversary. During the French Revolution an efficient mechanical contraption called guillotine was invented for beheading persons. These instances of seeking retributive justice demonstrate that perversity and cruelty are universal and spread across many cultures. In this connection it is worth pondering over the observation of noted writer VS Naipaul in his book 'Masque of Africa'. He explains cruel brutality of some recent authoritarian rulers of African states as continuity from the past where one tribe destroyed the other for dominance and even siblings were eliminated to ensure smooth and unchallenged seccession.

However, in our times, Armed Forces of civilised nations refrain from such revulsive behaviour for fear of international juridical reaction. Yet, non-state entities like terrorist groups at times mutilate the bodies of the dead in frenzied hatred and still worse, videograph these acts for display on media so as to strike fear in the hearts of those who oppose them. Progressive exploitation of civilian prisoners of war by the Nazi regime during the Second World War is a well known fact, but the revelations in the Memoirs of Carta-Del-Ponte (ex-chief prosecutor of war crimes in former Yugoslavia) shock our conscience by the heinousness of acts. She accuses Kosovan army of body harvesting of Serbian prisoners.

Apart from causing death and associated crimes, there are other offences committed by soldiers in the combat zone which violate human dignity. Offences like looting, rape, forced labour, prostitution and ill treatment of prisoners of war are quite common occurrences. Even if one believes that war is a gladiatorial sport, then there are no trophies for the victorious . Dispossessing civilians of their material belongings is theft. Soldiers do not commit theft to carry home war mementos. However in some instances captured military hardware or equipment may be turned over to authorities for accounting and preservation as 'war trophies' in public (institutional) custody. Capturing beautiful women, particularly those of royalty was in vogue since historical times, but forced prostitution on large scale is the legacy of the Second World War. It is as heinous a crime as ethnic cleansing and perpetuates socio-economic disorder for a long time after the crime. Penitent Japan apologised for the misdeeds of its armed forces nearly after fifty years.

'Prisoners of War' are usually the captured or surrendered members of adversary's armed forces. Yet, the expression POW is more generic than specific due to changing nature of war. There are conflict situations without formal declaration of war. In addition, certain categories of persons other than combatants are also accorded the status of POW by the liberal provisions of international regulations. Therefore, existence of conflict situation is adequate criterion for the purpose. Usually, ill-treatment of the POWs occur due to the following reasons:

a. The number of captured or surrendered prisoners is too large and logistic infrastructure in the war zone is inadequate to maintain them in accordance with international regulations.

b. Interrogation of prisoners using coercive methods to obtain tactical intellegence.

c. Due to retribution.

While the first is understandable, the second is untenable and the last is condemnable.

In this context, it is necessary to recollect the admirable conduct of the Indian Army in 1971 in East Pakistan (now Bangladesh). Nothing could have been more graceful than the treatment meted out to the Pakistani POWs who surrendered en block (nearly 93,000). In total contrast to this the treatment meted out to the POWs of Guantanamo Bay camp put the USA in an embarassing and shameful place.

The broad guideline for treatment of POWs may be summed up as - the honour of the individuals and human dignity should not be violated even though they are adversaries in conflict. The rights accorded to POWs by the International regulations are inalienable under all circumstances.

War and war making capability are multi-faceted activities. Some important facets are economy and trade, military industrial base and demography. It is common practice to attempt and cripple the enemy's war making capability even if destruction is not direct necessity for achievement of military objective. Some armies of bygone era practised scorched earth policy and Second World War ushered in the practice of carpet bombing of both civilian and military areas. British may thank Germans for a new London, it nevertheless was wanton destruction. The United States added the brutal edge to destruction by use of atomic bombs on Hiroshima and Nagasaki and Napalm bombs in Vietnam. The Americans justify the use of nuclear weapons on the premise of saving humanity from far greater atrocity. Despite precision guidance, propensity of modern munitions of war for widespread destruction precludes their reckless usage. Vast destruction, apart from wasting resources, may also trigger unprecedented ecological or environmental or demographical disasters too. The decision to use or otherwise, nuclear and chemical weapons is beyond tactical commander's domain, but their expertise must find unambiguous erxpression in their advice to the higher-ups in politico-military domain.

Destruction is at times motivated by reasons other than military objectives. Misguided religious zealotry prompts some combatants to indulge in iconoclasm. They vandalise objects and monuments having religious or cultural connotation.Reasons for such behaviour are at times apparent. For instance, idol worship is forbidden in religions like Islam. Such deep rooted beliefs and religious intolerance motivate them to vandalise these objects. Invading muslim armies of the middle ages have left permanent scars at cultural and religious heritage sites in India. However, it is deplorable that even while democratic and secular ideals are gaining momentum worldwide, there are fundamentalist organisations like Taliban who indulge in such vandalism. The world today recognises that cultural heritage is the common heritage of the mankind and need to be protected through national and international institutions and agencies. International law forbids destruction or vandalism of such sites by the military or any other combatants.

Whatever be the strategic or tactical objectives of war or conflict, it is the moral responsibility of the occupying or liberating force to ensure that dogs of war do not plunge the occupied or defeated country or territory into socio-economic turmoil or political abyss or human suffering. Even the withdrawal from the conflict may need to provide adequate time frame for smooth restoration to near normalcy. Failure to do so may result in aftermath being worse than the conflict itself. Here are some illustrative examples. When British gave up their rule of Indian sub continent in 1947 and partitioned it, half a million people were killed, twelve million displaced. When French gave up their long war in Algeria in 1962, France was inundated with refugees. The American withdrawals from Vietnam (1970s), Lebanon (1980s) and Somalia (1990s) were bitter experiences. Now, they face similar predicament in Iraq and Afghanistan. The probablity of occurrence of such situations is much higher in case of conflicts arising due to intervention than formally declared wars.

Intervention in pursuit of ideals of elite political ideology or in support of humanitarian causes or in execution of resolutions ratified by the world body (United Nations) may be justifiable but the process of withdrawal is nevertheless an onerous task. The prime requirement would be to ensure that some sort of functional government is in place. A jury government is often accused of being a stooge of the intervening power and therefore it may be necessary to establish its legitimacy through popular or democratic process. The process of establishing a political system and its taking roots is therefore a slow process. American counter insurgency specialist David Kilcullen aptly describes the process as 'marathon and not a sprint'. During the intervening period the probablity of law and order situation deteriorating and outbreak of civil war are very high. There is also urgent need to restore all civic amenities, particularly food supplies, shelter and critical healthcare facilities. Finally the reconstruction of war ravaged infrastructure, restoration of economy and industry are much slower and longer process but the cause of war should guide in determining responsibility for the same.

Basis of Combat Philosophy

> *"Western soldiers were victims of their own virtues, imbued since birth with all the decencies of their societies. The armies of totalitarian regimes are under no such restraint"*
>
> **- Max Hastings**
> **in *Armageddon***

Max Hastings is either naive or arrogant to assert that soldiers of western societies were embodiment of virtues while others were bereft of combat ethics. Actually most soldiers of civilised societies observed some form of ethical code but the basis of such code varied. What, then are the basis or value sources from which combat philosophy (code of conduct for soldiering in field) has evolved? Is it the political philosophy of the state? OR state religion? OR culture quotient of the society? OR any other set of customs and traditions? Earlier deliberations in this book on motives and nature of war suggest that any of the above or combination of these influences serve as the moral moorings in guiding the conduct of soldiers in the field. Awareness of these value systems provides the foundation for independent thinking and decision making by the soldiers in the field.

Military is an instrument in the hands of polity (political executive) for implementing state policy and therefore, it is only natural that their code of conduct is influenced by the political philosophy of the state they represent. For instance, the treatment meted out to prisoners of war by the military of a democratic state is likely to be humane while conduct of military of a state which aggressively advocates ethnic cleansing is likely to be brutal. A country waging a war from high moral stance is more likely to be responsible towards reconstruction and rehabilitation efforts in the aftermath of war.

Prevalence of terms like crusade, *jihad* and *dharma yuddha* indicate that societies past and present have at various times unabashedly advocated militant religious conduct leading to wars. In such circumstances behaviour of combatants is invariably influenced by their religion. However, in our times political communities prefer to use the expression 'clash of civilisations' to maintain diplomatic correctness in the comity of nations. Validity of the expression is debatable as civilizations do not clash, in fact, they collaborate, coalesce, assimilate and evolve. Religion has been both potent motivator and guiding light (code of conduct) to soldiers. Religious rites and practices abound in the armed forces of secular states too. As long as religion instills sobriety and sanity among soldiers there is no room for complaint, but when religion is misused to foster fundamentalism it deserves to be condemned. Religion itself can be used to promote secular and tolerant attitude.

The influence of cultural environment on the behaviour of combatants may not be specifically or distinctly evident but manifests in ways such as their obsession with customs and traditions. In instances where the forces are organised on martial race concept the influence is much more. The new members are indoctrinated about these values as part of induction and orientation training. These value systems have uncanny potential to motivate individuals into patriotic fervour. Brilliant examples of these can be found in the regimental system of the Indian Army and the kamikaze pilots of the erstwhile armed forces of Japan.

It would not be wrong to surmise that a soldier's behavioural responses under combat stress and battlefield conditions are influenced by multiple factors - political, socio-cultural and religious. Some factors are more dominant in particular societies. Yet, there can be no doubt about the appropriate basis for the code of conduct for the soldier of a modern nation state. It has to be the international humanitarian law which has universal approbation. A soldier's theology must spring from humanism, not from brutality or hatred; creativity not destructivity and sanity not insanity.

Laws of war

" The UN was not created to take mankind to heaven, but to save humanity from hell"

- Dag Hammarskjold
2nd Secretary General of UN

Emperor Asoka was disgusted with revulsive sight of death on the battlefield of Kalinga (255 BC) and renounced war and adopted peaceful doctrines of Buddhism. Much later, on the evening of the bloody battle of Solferino (1859 AD) Henry Dunant was aghast at the human suffering and he conceived the idea of Red Cross and international humanitarian law. His ideas expressed in his book *'A Memory of Solferino'* found favourable response in his own country Switzerland and the rest of Western society and formed the basis of humanitarian law. With passage of time propensity of war to cause widespread death and destruction has increased manifold due to development of higher weapons of war. If the evil face of war shocks our conscience too, then the evolution of regulatory mechanisms offer some semblance of hope and reassurance.

The growing complexity of modern war or armed conflicts has made the law of war so much more complicated that it is a massive body of nearly seven hundred provisions. These provisions of law are in the form of conventions and protocols. This entire body of legal provisions is based on two connected fundamental principles namely military necessity and humanity.

International Humanitarian Law evolved in two streams namely The Law of Geneva and The Law of the Hague. Both the streams developed concurrently but not as entirely separate. While the provisions of the former aim at protecting victims of armed conflict, the latter also called 'Law of War' has provisions to regulate conduct of military operations. Mere ratification by the nation states is not sufficient. They must demonstrate their will to observe them. Those responsible should be educated about these provisions or else violations become the norm and observance, the exception.

Chapter-11

Suicidal Missions

"It is the cause and not the death that makes the martyr"

- Napoleon Bonaparte

"The ink of the scholar and the blood of martyr are of equal value in heaven"

- Quran

"Let us all be brave enough to die the death of a martyr, but let no one lust for martyrdom"

- MK Gandhi

"The suicide bomber turns life itself into a horrible weapon"

- Micheal Hardt and Antonio Negri in '*Multitude*'

Visualisation of combat zone is incomplete without the emotional exhuberance of soldiers amidst death, destruction and disorder. Sanity and rationality often take backseat as frenzied soldiers indulge in acts some ignominious and others admirable. While the former are deemed war crimes and adequate provisions exist by way of their own law of the land and international law of war to deal with such gross perverse and degrading combat behaviour, this chapter proposes to deliberate on the single most important and often admired extreme combat behaviour that is frequently referred to as suicidal mission.

The quotes above (there are many more) demonstrate the possibility of different perspectives of the practice. This practice or method is adopted by widely diverse groups - practitioners of both regular and irregular forms of warfare; by the soldiers of secular states and religious warriors of nonstate entities and by the soldiers of democratic states as well as oppressive regimes of governance. Wide spread preference for this extreme combat behaviour is understandable. Suicidal missions have the potential to subdue otherwise invincible targets and can achieve disproportionately favourable results by overcoming numerically or technologically superior adversary. Human precision, determination and reliability provide cutting edge to this method. It is often adopted as the last resort in the face of imminent defeat. The method has great appeal for the practitoners of irregular warfare, particularly the non-state entities with limited resources. Psychologically too, it can shock and demoralise a competant adversary. Not withstanding the efficacy of the method, there are ethical issues that need to be addressed and resolved in peacetime – far from the deafening din of the battlefield and frenzied war cries of the soldiers. Studies of combat behaviour with psychological bias are useful in evaluating mental health and motivational levels of combatants. Shifting the bias to ethical and legal aspects helps in determining the societal attitude – approbation or otherwise of such actions by soldiers in combat zone. However, the whole range of studies or deliberations are unlikely to produce a 'phenotype', but will certainly enhance our understanding of this select extreme combat behavioural practice. This writing attempts to synthesise various attitudes into a coherent (to the possible extent) stream of understanding.

An appropriate starting point for speculative deliberation on the subject is perhaps the lexicon of the composite expression itself. Suicide is a voluntary and deliberate act of terminating one's own life. For obvious reasons such actions have neither religious nor legal sanction in most societies, religious groups or political communities. A lot of negativity is also associated with the act and failed attempt is punishable. The word mission suggests dedicated pursuit of higher objective or cause. The two words coalesce and in the process the former gains acceptability as self sacrifice and latter gains approbation and admiration as a noble cause. How much ever eulogised the practice may be, suicidal action by a soldier seems antithetical to a rational mind. What psychological reasons or motives prompt a soldier, who has been trained to act violently towards his adversary, to give up his own life voluntarily? Or is his self destruction (suicidal action) in order to destroy his adversary a violent action in itself? Attempts to unravel motivational aspects of this extreme behaviour have drawn a blank. For instance, investigators scanned the last letters written by the Kamikaze pilots (the single largest group of volunteers who undertook suicidal missions) to their near and dear ones. An enigmatic poignancy pervades but no answers come forth.

However based on circumstantial corroboration certain generalisations on this extreme combat behaviour are possible.

a. Suicidal missions are usually adopted as the instrument of last resort when faced with imminent defeat or all other options have been frustrated. For non-state entities like terrorist organisations this may be the normal mode.

b. Practitioners of suicidal missions are usually committed to some kind of value system based on religion, culture, political idealogy or customs and traditions. Islamic jihadists believe that martyrs are rewarded in heaven. Some oriental religious beliefs that living and death are part of the same continuum makes death easily acceptable. The Samurai are guided by bushido (code of the warrior) which stresses the willingness to die as necessary. Extreme loyalty to the head of state or political ideology may be in vogue. Organisational customs and traditions like regiments and other combat units may induce individuals to follow the past examples.

c. When volunteers are sought, group or peer pressure (direct or indirect) may compel individuals to accept the role rather than stand apart.

Having dwelt upon the working and motivational aspects of this extreme combat behaviour, the deliberations need to veer to the most important concern - the ethical dimension. Can this method be regarded as a tactic or just stray incidents of extreme behaviour by frenzied soldiers? Regarding it as a tactic would mean official acquiescence of the ethos of suicidal missions. Most widely known precedent of such attitude is that of the Japanese naval high command which officially sanctioned suicidal missions in the form of Kamikaze pilots. However, such extremely cruel tactics are not easily acceptable to the western mind and for valid reasons too. Death of combatants in the combat zone is a distinct high probability and certain categories of personnel like infantry soldiers and those employed on mine clearance at the forefront, pilots and frogmen on clandestine missions face even much higher risks. Although the soldiers of a good fighting force are ever willing to make the supreme sacrifice, yet death of combatants can not be presupposed. Therefore, it behoves on any authority inducting a soldier into any situation to ensure that the individual has a chance of coming out alive - at least a slim one if not a fair one. It is for this reason that suicidal missions have to be spontaneous and voluntary. It has also to be individual decision and not an organised activity. It would not be grossly incorrect to regard external motivation to undertake suicidal missions as abetment to suicide.

The ethical stance that the armed forces of a secular democracy should adopt has been stated above in an unambiguous manner. Organising or suggestion of suicidal missions as a tactic is unacceptable to the military ethos of a democracy. Having enunciated the code, there is a need to examine the functional modalities in our armed forces. India, like other countries in the world, has created some special forces (part of armed forces) that are trained to undertake challenging and risky tasks that require specialised skills, mental strength and extraordinary physical courage. They are also highly motivated personnel. Indian Army has a special force created under the parachute regiment. The Indian Navy has a marine commando wing. It is important that while designating these forces, their motto and insignia should avoid any suggestion of suicidal missions. The special forces of the Indian Army has a insignia on which the word 'balidaan' is inscribed.

Finally, there are certain societal obligations towards these forces. They quite often operate behind enemy lines or territory during prehostilities (prior to formal declaration of war) period and indulge in clandenstine activities. It is unethical for any government to disown these soldiers merely to avoid diplomatic embarassment. Still worse is the denial of service benefits to the next of kin.

Part- 4

Other related issues

Part IV - Other related issues

Chapter 12: Influence of demographics on recruitment

Chapter 13: Indigenisation of Indian armed forces

Chapter 14: National ethos and defence

Chapter-12

Influence of demographics on recruitment

Not withstanding the status enjoyed by the military as an institution and its members, demographics of a society have profound influence on the recruitment policy and process of the armed forces. The term recruitment is used in a generic way in this writing and includes both officers and men. Societies which are sparsely populated or face difficulties in recruiting suitable manpower in adequate numbers have at times resorted to extreme measures like conscription, removing the gender barrier and offering citizenship to non-nationals enrolled. Size of the population is not the only criterion. Some aspects of the Indian demography like ethnicity, religion, language, gender and political correctness have been discussed in earlier chapters. In this chapter effects of socio-economic changes, education and development on the recruitment process are deliberated upon. Limitations of training capacities of institutions have only accentuated the problem.

India's achievements in post independance period in areas like education, industrialisation, employment opportunities and socio-political awareness may be regarded as significant. This transformation has brought about paradigm shifts in both societal and individual attitudes. For instance, shifting societal attitude towards growing population is most discernible through paradigms—population explosion, reservoir of manpower, human resource, human capital (assets). Similarly individual attitudes, aspirations, expectations and value system stand transformed. Armed forces prospecting for suitable human resource will have to take cognizance of transformed socio-cultural environment.

Education in Indian constitutional context is a concurrent subject. Concerted efforts by both central and federal system and also by private enterprise have resulted in expanded educational infrastructure and facilities. The final outcome has been a vast reservoir of educated manpower. Aggressive industrialisation policy implemented through public and private sectors has increased employment opportunities manifold. Globalisation of economy has not only enhanced these opportunities but also made them monetarily attractive. The resultant economic affluence and education have led to greater socio-political awareness.

While the military establishment can prospect

this vast reservoir for suitable manpower, it may also in some instances be able to reduce the initial training effort, but the flip side is that the prospective candidates also tend to evaluate a career option in the armed forces in a pragmatic and material (socio-economic considerations) manner. Once a decade revision of salary, professional risks and hazards, long term commitment and rigid service conditions do not constitute an attractive career option. Due to paradigm shift in value system, individuals may not opt for career in defence services as a martial or familial tradition as was prevalent in yester years.

The military establishment in India routinely admits shortfalls in staffing and recruitment. The problem needs to be tackled on two fronts. Cost of manpower will increase with improvement in socio-economic conditions. It is, therefore, advisable to introduce automation and induct superior technology. This aspect is beyond the scope of this chapter. The other aspect is to view manpower recruitment process in contemporary socio-economic and cultural context. Aggressive prospecting in the recent past by the military establishment is discernible through attractive advertisements in both print and visual media, yet they overlook an important avenue close to them-veterans (ex-servicemen). They are the most effective and impressive ambassadors of the armed forces. Yet, it needs to be noted with concern that the number of second generation entrants is dwindling. One possible speculation is that the recruitment process to some extent exploits the gullible which is undesirable.

The way forward to make military career attractive

and satisfying to individuals as also build up institutional image is to change service conditions (regulations, functional methods and practices) to be in consonance with political philosophy of state (constitution) and societal norms. Conditions of service in military are tough due to professional requirements but should not be aggravated by whimsical misinterpretation. It is not possible to consider the entire gamut of service conditions in this brief writing. Only some demonstative instances are narrated. During the bygone years, personnel were curtailed or denied of their entitled leave, study leave and joining time on transfer at the whims and fancies of superiors. It is surprising that personnel are being granted full entitled leave ever since the government approved encashment of leave. Study leave, unheard of in earlier days has become a common place subsequent to cadre review resulting in dearth of billets to accomodate promoted officers. Inadequate provision of accomodation for personnel is aggravated by societal shift towards nuclear family. Thoughtless scheduling of exercises during examinations of children, festival season and over the weekends create avoidable discomfort to individuals and families. It is ridiculous that the armed forces wait for circumstantial compulsions or disgruntlement to reach a fervant state to change their attitude. The armed forces are compelled to discharge from service a large number of personnel on regular basis due to compulsions of hierarchical structure and to maintain youthful profile of the armed forces. Discharging these personnel into wilderness of unemployment is not only lack of concern for personnel but also waste of well trained manpower. The government should accept rehabilitation of discharged personnel as its obligation instead of treating it as a welfare measure.

There are some abominable practices that have been in vogue since colonial times. Only those practices which are in consonance with egalitarian democratic norms may be retained. Putting an end to undesirable practices may seem like loss of time or established privileges to some persons, but they need to be sensitised about getting rid of those practices in the larger interests of service. Demeaning practices in the armed forces are not deliberated upon here, lest it be perceived as an attempt to spread disenchantment amongst personnel. Touchstone to test the acceptability of any practice is that it should not undermine the dignity of the individuals or the image of the institution.

Human resource management processes of recruitment, retention and rehabilitation should be in consonance with socio-political environment.

Chapter-13

Indigenisation of Indian armed forces

We, the people of India are inclined to believe that our country is an emerging economic and military power- not through any learned conviction but because the rest of the world tells us so. The chief determinants of military power are, size and capabilities of the armed forces; physical and economic sustainability of that force; political will to exploit military as an instrument of strategic assertion in international relations and the level of indigenisation of armed forces. Any acquisition or induction of major military hardware triggers either accolades or lament about the indigenisation process and performance of the involved agencies. Yet, the usual rhetoric carries no intelligence for the ordinary citizen. This writing attempts to facilitate better understanding of indigenisation.

There is a vague awareness about Research and Development (R & D), Production and Engineering (E). Therefore, definable clarity of R&D & E process train is useful. Research is evaluation and feasibility analysis of potential technologies for implementation/adoption in current and future products. Research mode has two streams namely, fundamental and applied. There are occasions when the fundamental research may require to abandon futile projects as also pursue new technologies/areas that the researchers may chance upon. It is for this reason that fundamental research has loosely constructed time frame while applied research has fixed time frame. Development is translation of feasible technologies into user acceptable product(s) for implementation in production stream.

Adherence to time frame deadlines is very important in defence R&D endeavours so that it results in worthwhile and useful products. Engineering includes failure analysis and continuous product improvement. The above definitions need to be translated into the Indian DRDO context. The threshold of academic excellence in our elite institutions of higher learning is adequate enough to obviate fundamenal research by DRDO (except in case of a few selected areas.) Therefore, the functional domain of DRDO is applied research and product development. Engineering in case of defence equipment assumes the form of field trials and equipment performance evaluation.

Defence R&D&E process train has to meet certain stringent demands in terms of time frames, quality considerations and compatibility. Viewed under such a regime, failure of Indian DRDO is undeniable ground reality, despite the platitudes mouthed by its chiefs who at times masquerade as visionaries. The only response to their citing stray incidents of success is 'single swallow does not maketh a summer'.

The need is to examine the maladies that afflict the indigenisation process with honesty of purpose. While it may not be prudent to impose rigid time frames on the regime, the Indian DRDO and defence related PSU's function as if they are working towards obsolescence. Such tardy functioning results in not only cost escalation but also the armed forces who have been denied acquisitions from foreign sources are left ill-equipped adversely affecting their operational capabilities. Long term force planning is also rendered ineffective as acquisitions from foreign sources too have long lead time. India missed the industrial revolution, however, the first Prime Minister Nehru was believer and advocate of Industrialisation even in the face of staunch (adamant) opposition from Gandhi. Yet, India in the past six decades has demonstrated socio-cultural inability to quickly absorb technology. Therefore, there has been not much finesse achieved in product development or production. Then there is the product compatibility criterion. Products of defence R&D cannot be regarded as complete in themselves. They will have to fit into the whole scheme of integration into platforms and be in consonance with operational and maintenance ethos. Unfortunately, the Indian military establishment itself has not developed any coherent operational or maintenance ethos. Modest ethos that may exist is borrowed from those political communities (nations) that have supplied military hardware. Infact assimilating and integrating the disparate into a homogenous unity has been a big challenge. Such situation is not conducive to indigenisation, operation, training or maintenance.

The causes for poor performance of DRDO and the defence related PSU's are easily discernible. There are large number of individuals in this domain wearing twin hats with divided loyalties. For instance, the chief of DRDO is also the scientific adviser to the prime minister. There are also service/retired defence officers/bureaucrats employed in defence related PSU's. These individuals instead of contributing their technical and administrative expertise, attempt to sweep failures and poor performance under the carpet. Lack of accountability is carried to the very literal level of following cost plus method.

When indigenisation through self help and evolving a culture of excellence have failed, there are other methods of achieving transfer of technology and manufacturing excellence. The two main routes are Offsets and Foreign Direct Investment (FDI). However, these methods have not been rationally exploited due to an attitude of over cautiousness about corruption, compromise of security and flight of capital. The remedy lies in optimising the processes and minimising the ill effects.

Chapter-14

National ethos and defence

This chapter contains concluding reflections on the functioning of national security mechanism in India. For reasons of coherence it recapitulates certain salients of historical background that have shaped Indian attitude towards national security; unsatisfactory working of institutional interfaces and other defence related issues.

Deliberations on nationhood provide the appropriate context for appreciation of national security concerns. Ancient Indian civilisation demonstrated voracious capacity for assimilation and at times it was even enriching but there are subtle distinctions between a nation and civilisation. A nation state is usually a well defined geographical entity whose political philosophy is enshrined in its constitutional framework and has dedicated institutions to uphold constitution. It is a viable and sustainable economic entity. A nation adopts a foreign policy to promote its multifarious interests in the comity or hegemony of nations. A defence policy delineates and guides the build up and operation of armed forces, primarily to ensure territorial integrity but also to serve as the last resort instrument for implementing state policy. All institutions of the state have working interfaces between them. However, the intrinsic relationship between sovereign nationhood and defence is crucial so much so that they may be regarded as conjoined twins. Any attempt to separate them is fraught with mortal risk to either or both.

India assumed geographical configuration resembling the present day reality only after independence in 1947 with ill delineated international borders. The result was that the country was born in a hostile neighbourhood with contesting claims to territory. Internally too, the country was non homogenous amalgam of erstwhile states. The much touted ' unity amidst diversity' turned out to be a fallacy. On the contrary, diversity of ethnicity, religion and language has led to fissures ranging from attempts at secession; seeking regional autonomy; sub division of federal states to empathy with trans national groups. This internal diversity has also created identifiable vote banks (prime objective of Indian polity) and growth of regional political outfits. Selective agendas of these outfits in federal states are on many occassions at variance with national objectives leading to responses varying from non cooperation to vehement opposition to the central government. The situation assumes gravity as the armed forces are involved in maintaining internal security over large areas of the country or are deployed as instrument of state policy abroad.

If that was geographical and political affront to evolution of nationalistic ethos, the historical circumstances were no less unfavourable. Leaders of nationalist movement were partially exposed to administrative process through limited self rule even prior to independence but defence and foreign policy domains remained imperial subjects beyond the purview of nationalist leaders. Leaders like Nehru and Gandhi relegated national security due to ignorance; lack of understanding of international relations and overconfidence in their own standing as statesmen and idealism. They could not comprehend the difference between their non-violent struggle for independence and proactive defence as a state obligation. The polity, therefore, chose to regard military as an unavoidable appendage of a modern nation state. The framers of Indian Constitution too failed to accord institutional status to the body military thus reducing its status to that of a department of Government of India to be supervised by bureaucracy. On the other hand, bureaucracy which is only a part and lower echelon of working of political executive managed to achieve the exalted status for their role as interlocutor between ignorant polity and professional military. In similar vein the erstwhile civil service (ICS) had rendered the nascent foreign policy mechanism (IFS) into a still born entity. The outcome has been a disaster. India has had no worthwhile defence or foreign policy mechanisms.

Under such circumstances lack of inheritance in strategic thinking or planning was perhaps inevitable. Whether it is military operations or managing security environment or force planning, the Indian response has always been reactive ad-hocism. It is all the more disappointing that in seven decades of the post independence period no proactive effort has been made to develop strategic culture or planning. India has fought several wars and on most occasions it was either loss of territory or loss of strategic advantage. It is a poor consolation that the lost territory was either sandy desert of Rajasthan or the snow covered Himalayan heights where not a blade of grass grows. Pragmatic settlement of international territorial disputes through negotiations has not been possible due to lack of diplomatic resoluteness and constitutional constraints (territorial bargaining tantamounts to constitutional amendment). India today survives in a hostile environment, even erstwhile friendly nations have been alienated due to faulty or unsuccessful foreign policy.

Force planning or acquisition process has been ad-hoc due to sporadic instances of corruption in arms procurement and failure of the indigenisation process, thus leaving the armed forces ill equipped. Indian nuclear aspirations may well come to nought due to incoherent nuclear policy, state of arsenal and lack of reliable command and control infrastructure. Hollow idealism of 'no first use' in a world of militant nationalism is self deprecatory and serves no purpose but devalues deterrence (very purpose of nuclear capabality). State of nuclear arsenal, where demated parts are held in custody of two antagonistic agencies and absence of credible command and control structure which can coordinate the tasks of the nuclear triad will ensure that even a retaliatory strike is not possible. Even in a conventional war, the existing Indian mechanism for higher direction of war is not efficient to meet the demands of present day warfare, particularly with regard to speed and joint warfare. All that can be said at this juncture is that outcome of any future wars may not be favourable to India if remedial measures are not initiated at this stage.

The cost of manpower, the most important resource for defence, is ever escalating due to multiple reasons, but the situation is both an opportunity and challenge. A country like India which prides itself for having the second largest Army, fourth largest Air Force and seventh largest Navy must identify an opportunity to downsize without adversely affecting operational efficiency. There are two effective methods of achieving this objective—harnessing technology and creation of reserve of manpower which can be embodied at short notice. We do have territorial army and a youth service called National Cadet Corps. The requirement is to streamline the methodology for mobilisation. It is not merely mobilisation of manpower resources that should be established but also other aspects. War is an all embracing national activity for which the entire nation needs to be mobilised. The past endeavours in this direction have not been successful.

There are some issues like customs and traditions of the armed forces which seem trivial but are important from point of maintenance of discipline and morale. These need to be respected. For instance the armed forces have adopted western mode of dressing due to functional suitability. There are some defence ministers who choose to wear loincloth or pyjamas in defence environment. After all, the defence minister is the chief executive of the armed forces and such insensitivity earns them disdain of uniformed fraternity. There is a need to develop national ethos which respects the armed forces and their role. It is the foundation of healthy inter institutional relationship in a democracy. It also nurtures elitism among the armed forces.

Epilogue

"Ours is a world of nuclear giants and ethical infants"

- Omar Bradley
US General

Ernst Mayr, a great biologist of our times estimated that of about fifty billion species since origin of life only one achieved the kind of intelligence needed to establish a civilisation. It did so perhaps 100,000 years ago. He also made the sombre observation that average life expectancy of a species is about 100,000 years. Reflecting on the above observation Noam Chomsky, a political writer in his book *'Hegemony or Survival'* suggests that humans were a kind of 'biological error' using their allotted time to destroy each other and much else. Recurrence of wars at alarming frequency and their growing sinisterness compels us to believe that Chomksy's apprehensions are not unfounded.

Nuclear proliferation continues unabated propelled by scientific advances and technological developments. Warfare is spreading in to diverse areas like space, climatology and bacteriology. Smart robots and autonomous drones are entering the combat zone. Military philosophy is not a rigid or static body of modalities. It evolves in consonance with demands of the nature of warfare.

The modicum of hope stems from sanity and restraint of statesmen and soldiers.

Index